55 Peanut Butter Recipes for Home

By: Kelly Johnson

Table of Contents

- Classic Peanut Butter Cookies
- Peanut Butter Banana Smoothie
- Peanut Butter Energy Bites
- Peanut Butter and Jelly Sandwich
- Peanut Butter Fudge
- Peanut Butter Chocolate Chip Pancakes
- Thai Peanut Noodles
- Peanut Butter Cupcakes
- Peanut Butter Granola Bars
- Peanut Butter and Banana Bread
- Peanut Butter Hummus
- Peanut Butter Chocolate Milkshake
- Peanut Butter Oatmeal Cookies
- Peanut Butter and Jelly Thumbprint Cookies
- Peanut Butter Swirl Brownies
- Peanut Butter Cheesecake
- Peanut Butter Banana Muffins
- Peanut Butter Ice Cream
- Peanut Butter Pretzel Bites
- Peanut Butter Cup Smoothie Bowl
- Peanut Butter and Chocolate Tart
- Peanut Butter and Honey Toast
- Peanut Butter Cup Cookies
- Peanut Butter Protein Balls
- Thai Peanut Chicken Satay
- Peanut Butter Cup Cheesecake Bars
- Peanut Butter and Chocolate Truffles
- Peanut Butter Banana Bread Pudding
- Peanut Butter and Chocolate Pretzel Bark
- Peanut Butter Rice Krispie Treats
- Peanut Butter and Jelly Oat Bars
- Peanut Butter Cup Milkshake
- Peanut Butter Banana Pancakes
- Peanut Butter Granola
- Peanut Butter and Chocolate Mousse

- Peanut Butter Cup Brownie Bites
- Peanut Butter Banana Ice Cream
- Peanut Butter and Jelly Cupcakes
- Peanut Butter and Chocolate Pie
- Peanut Butter and Pretzel Pie
- Peanut Butter and Jelly Smoothie
- Peanut Butter Cup Popcorn
- Peanut Butter and Chocolate Stuffed French Toast
- Peanut Butter Cup Cookie Bars
- Peanut Butter and Banana Smoothie Bowl
- Peanut Butter Cup Mug Cake
- Peanut Butter and Jelly Cheesecake
- Peanut Butter and Chocolate Covered Strawberries
- Peanut Butter Cup Waffles
- Peanut Butter and Jelly Overnight Oats
- Peanut Butter and Chocolate Popsicles
- Peanut Butter Cup Ice Cream Cake
- Peanut Butter and Banana Quesadilla
- Peanut Butter Cup Cheesecake Brownies
- Peanut Butter and Chocolate Pudding

Classic Peanut Butter Cookies

Ingredients:

- 1 cup unsalted butter, softened
- 1 cup granulated sugar
- 1 cup packed brown sugar
- 2 large eggs
- 1 cup creamy peanut butter
- 1 teaspoon vanilla extract
- 3 cups all-purpose flour
- 1 teaspoon baking powder
- 1/2 teaspoon baking soda
- 1/2 teaspoon salt
- Additional granulated sugar for rolling (optional)

Instructions:

Preheat the Oven:
- Preheat your oven to 350°F (175°C). Line baking sheets with parchment paper.

Cream Butter and Sugars:
- In a large mixing bowl, cream together softened butter, granulated sugar, and brown sugar until light and fluffy.

Add Eggs and Peanut Butter:
- Add eggs one at a time, beating well after each addition. Mix in creamy peanut butter and vanilla extract until well combined.

Combine Dry Ingredients:
- In a separate bowl, whisk together the all-purpose flour, baking powder, baking soda, and salt.

Mix Wet and Dry Ingredients:
- Gradually add the dry ingredients to the peanut butter mixture, mixing just until combined. Do not overmix.

Shape Cookies:
- Scoop tablespoon-sized portions of dough and roll them into balls. If desired, roll each ball in additional granulated sugar for a slightly crunchy exterior.

Make Crosshatch Pattern:

- Place the cookie dough balls onto the prepared baking sheets. Use a fork to make a crisscross pattern on each cookie, gently flattening them.

Bake:
- Bake in the preheated oven for 10-12 minutes or until the edges are golden brown.

Cool:
- Allow the cookies to cool on the baking sheets for a few minutes before transferring them to a wire rack to cool completely.

Enjoy:
- Once cooled, enjoy these classic Peanut Butter Cookies with a glass of milk or your favorite beverage!

These cookies are simple to make and have that irresistible combination of a crunchy exterior and a soft, chewy interior.

Peanut Butter Banana Smoothie

Ingredients:

- 1 ripe banana, peeled and sliced
- 1 cup milk (dairy or plant-based)
- 2 tablespoons creamy peanut butter
- 1 tablespoon honey or maple syrup (optional, for sweetness)
- 1/2 teaspoon vanilla extract
- 1/2 cup Greek yogurt or a frozen banana for added creaminess
- Ice cubes (optional)

Instructions:

Prepare Ingredients:
- Ensure the banana is ripe and sliced.

Blend:
- In a blender, combine the sliced banana, milk, creamy peanut butter, honey (if using), vanilla extract, and Greek yogurt or frozen banana.

Blend Until Smooth:
- Blend on high speed until the ingredients are well combined and the smoothie reaches your desired consistency.

Adjust Thickness:
- If the smoothie is too thick, you can add more milk. If it's too thin, you can add more banana or ice cubes.

Taste and Adjust Sweetness:
- Taste the smoothie and adjust the sweetness by adding more honey or maple syrup if desired.

Serve:
- Pour the Peanut Butter Banana Smoothie into a glass.

Optional Garnish:
- Garnish with a drizzle of peanut butter on top or a sprinkle of crushed peanuts.

Enjoy:
- Enjoy this delicious and protein-packed Peanut Butter Banana Smoothie as a nutritious breakfast or a satisfying snack!

Feel free to customize this smoothie by adding a handful of spinach for a green boost or a scoop of protein powder for an extra protein kick.

Peanut Butter Energy Bites

Ingredients:

- 1 cup old-fashioned oats
- 1/2 cup creamy peanut butter
- 1/3 cup honey or maple syrup
- 1 cup shredded coconut (sweetened or unsweetened)
- 1/2 cup ground flaxseed
- 1 teaspoon vanilla extract
- A pinch of salt
- Optional: 1/2 cup chocolate chips or chopped nuts

Instructions:

Combine Dry Ingredients:
- In a large bowl, combine old-fashioned oats, shredded coconut, ground flaxseed, and a pinch of salt.

Add Wet Ingredients:
- Add creamy peanut butter, honey or maple syrup, and vanilla extract to the dry ingredients.

Mix Well:
- Mix all the ingredients until well combined. If the mixture is too dry, you can add a bit more peanut butter or honey.

Optional Add-ins:
- If desired, fold in chocolate chips or chopped nuts for added texture and flavor.

Chill the Mixture:
- Place the mixture in the refrigerator for about 30 minutes. Chilling makes it easier to shape into balls.

Shape into Bites:
- Once chilled, take small portions of the mixture and roll them into bite-sized balls using your hands.

Store:
- Place the Peanut Butter Energy Bites on a parchment-lined tray or plate.

Chill Again (Optional):
- If you prefer firmer bites, you can chill them in the refrigerator for an additional 15-30 minutes.

Enjoy:
- Once they are firm, your Peanut Butter Energy Bites are ready to eat! Store any leftovers in an airtight container in the refrigerator.

These energy bites are perfect for a quick and nutritious snack, providing a good balance of healthy fats, fiber, and protein.

Peanut Butter and Jelly Sandwich

Ingredients:

- 2 slices of bread (whole wheat, white, or your preference)
- 2 tablespoons peanut butter (creamy or crunchy)
- 1-2 tablespoons jelly or jam (grape, strawberry, raspberry, etc.)

Instructions:

Spread Peanut Butter:
- Take one slice of bread and spread a layer of peanut butter evenly over the entire surface. Use as much or as little as you prefer.

Add Jelly or Jam:
- Spoon jelly or jam onto the second slice of bread. Spread it evenly over the entire surface.

Assemble the Sandwich:
- Place the slice with peanut butter on top of the slice with jelly, creating a sandwich.

Press Together:
- Press the two slices together, ensuring that the peanut butter and jelly sides are facing each other.

Cut (Optional):
- Optionally, you can cut the sandwich into halves or quarters for easier handling.

Enjoy:
- Your Peanut Butter and Jelly Sandwich is ready to be enjoyed! Pair it with a glass of milk or your favorite beverage.

Feel free to customize your sandwich by experimenting with different types of bread, nut butters, or fruit spreads. It's a quick and classic choice for lunch, snacks, or a simple meal on the go.

Peanut Butter Fudge

Ingredients:

- 2 cups granulated sugar
- 1/2 cup unsalted butter
- 1/2 cup whole milk
- 1 cup creamy peanut butter
- 1 teaspoon vanilla extract
- 3 cups powdered sugar

Instructions:

Prepare Pan:
- Line an 8-inch square baking pan with parchment paper, leaving an overhang on the sides for easy removal.

Combine Sugar, Butter, and Milk:
- In a medium saucepan, combine granulated sugar, unsalted butter, and milk. Cook over medium heat, stirring constantly, until the mixture comes to a boil. Allow it to boil for 2-3 minutes without stirring.

Remove from Heat:
- Remove the saucepan from heat.

Add Peanut Butter and Vanilla:
- Stir in creamy peanut butter and vanilla extract until well combined.

Add Powdered Sugar:
- Gradually add the powdered sugar, mixing well until smooth and no lumps remain.

Pour into Pan:
- Pour the fudge mixture into the prepared baking pan, spreading it evenly.

Chill:
- Place the pan in the refrigerator and let the fudge chill for at least 2-3 hours, or until it is set.

Cut into Squares:
- Once set, lift the fudge out of the pan using the parchment paper overhang. Place it on a cutting board and cut into squares.

Serve:
- Serve the Peanut Butter Fudge at room temperature and enjoy!

This easy Peanut Butter Fudge recipe results in a creamy and indulgent treat that's perfect for satisfying your sweet tooth.

Peanut Butter Chocolate Chip Pancakes

Ingredients:

- 1 cup all-purpose flour
- 2 tablespoons sugar
- 1 teaspoon baking powder
- 1/2 teaspoon baking soda
- 1/4 teaspoon salt
- 3/4 cup buttermilk
- 1/4 cup milk
- 1/2 cup creamy peanut butter
- 1 large egg
- 2 tablespoons unsalted butter, melted
- 1/2 cup chocolate chips
- Additional butter for cooking
- Maple syrup for serving

Instructions:

Preheat Griddle or Pan:
- Preheat a griddle or non-stick pan over medium heat.

Mix Dry Ingredients:
- In a large bowl, whisk together the all-purpose flour, sugar, baking powder, baking soda, and salt.

Combine Wet Ingredients:
- In another bowl, whisk together buttermilk, milk, creamy peanut butter, egg, and melted butter until well combined.

Combine Wet and Dry Ingredients:
- Pour the wet ingredients into the dry ingredients and stir until just combined. Do not overmix; a few lumps are okay.

Add Chocolate Chips:
- Gently fold in the chocolate chips into the pancake batter.

Cook Pancakes:
- Lightly grease the griddle or pan with butter. Pour 1/4 cup portions of batter onto the hot surface.

Cook Until Bubbles Form:

- Cook until bubbles form on the surface of the pancakes and the edges begin to look set.

Flip and Cook Other Side:
- Flip the pancakes and cook the other side until golden brown.

Repeat:
- Repeat until all the batter is used.

Serve:
- Serve the Peanut Butter Chocolate Chip Pancakes warm, stacked, and drizzled with maple syrup.

Feel free to customize these pancakes by adding sliced bananas, chopped nuts, or a dollop of whipped cream on top. Enjoy your delightful breakfast treat!

Thai Peanut Noodles

Ingredients:

For the Sauce:

- 1/4 cup creamy peanut butter
- 3 tablespoons soy sauce
- 2 tablespoons lime juice
- 2 tablespoons rice vinegar
- 1 tablespoon sesame oil
- 2 tablespoons honey or maple syrup
- 1 garlic clove, minced
- 1 teaspoon grated ginger
- 1 teaspoon sriracha sauce (adjust to taste)
- 2 tablespoons warm water (to thin the sauce)

For the Noodles:

- 8 ounces rice noodles or any other noodles of your choice
- 1 tablespoon vegetable oil
- 1 red bell pepper, thinly sliced
- 1 carrot, julienned
- 1 cup broccoli florets, blanched
- 1/2 cup sliced green onions (scallions)
- Sesame seeds and chopped peanuts for garnish (optional)
- Fresh cilantro for garnish

Instructions:

Prepare the Sauce:
- In a bowl, whisk together peanut butter, soy sauce, lime juice, rice vinegar, sesame oil, honey or maple syrup, minced garlic, grated ginger, sriracha, and warm water. Adjust the consistency by adding more warm water if needed. Set aside.

Cook the Noodles:

- Cook the rice noodles according to the package instructions. Drain and rinse under cold water to stop the cooking process. Toss with a bit of oil to prevent sticking.

Sauté Vegetables:
- In a large skillet or wok, heat vegetable oil over medium heat. Add sliced red bell pepper, julienned carrot, and blanched broccoli florets. Sauté for 3-4 minutes until the vegetables are tender-crisp.

Combine Noodles and Sauce:
- Add the cooked noodles to the skillet with the sautéed vegetables. Pour the prepared peanut sauce over the noodles and vegetables.

Toss to Coat:
- Toss everything together, ensuring that the noodles and vegetables are well coated with the sauce. Cook for an additional 2-3 minutes to heat through.

Garnish and Serve:
- Remove from heat and garnish with sliced green onions, sesame seeds, chopped peanuts, and fresh cilantro.

Serve Warm:
- Serve the Thai Peanut Noodles warm. You can also squeeze additional lime juice over the top if desired.

These Thai Peanut Noodles are flavorful, satisfying, and can be customized with your favorite vegetables or protein. Enjoy!

Peanut Butter Cupcakes

Ingredients:

For the Cupcakes:

- 1 and 1/2 cups all-purpose flour
- 1 and 1/2 teaspoons baking powder
- 1/2 teaspoon baking soda
- 1/4 teaspoon salt
- 1/2 cup unsalted butter, softened
- 1/2 cup granulated sugar
- 1/2 cup brown sugar, packed
- 2 large eggs
- 1 teaspoon vanilla extract
- 3/4 cup buttermilk

For the Peanut Butter Frosting:

- 1 cup creamy peanut butter
- 1/2 cup unsalted butter, softened
- 2 cups powdered sugar
- 1/4 cup milk
- 1 teaspoon vanilla extract
- Pinch of salt

Optional Toppings:

- Chopped peanuts or mini chocolate chips for garnish

Instructions:

For the Cupcakes:

Preheat Oven:
- Preheat your oven to 350°F (175°C). Line a muffin tin with cupcake liners.

Combine Dry Ingredients:
- In a medium bowl, whisk together flour, baking powder, baking soda, and salt. Set aside.

Cream Butter and Sugars:

- In a large mixing bowl, cream together softened butter, granulated sugar, and brown sugar until light and fluffy.

Add Eggs and Vanilla:
- Add the eggs one at a time, beating well after each addition. Stir in the vanilla extract.

Alternate Adding Dry Ingredients and Buttermilk:
- Gradually add the dry ingredients to the wet ingredients, alternating with the buttermilk. Begin and end with the dry ingredients, mixing until just combined.

Fill Cupcake Liners:
- Divide the batter evenly among the cupcake liners, filling each about 2/3 full.

Bake:
- Bake in the preheated oven for 18-20 minutes or until a toothpick inserted into the center comes out clean. Allow cupcakes to cool in the tin for a few minutes before transferring them to a wire rack to cool completely.

For the Peanut Butter Frosting:

Beat Peanut Butter and Butter:
- In a large bowl, beat together creamy peanut butter and softened butter until smooth.

Add Powdered Sugar and Milk:
- Gradually add powdered sugar, milk, vanilla extract, and a pinch of salt. Beat until well combined and creamy.

Frost Cupcakes:
- Once the cupcakes are completely cooled, frost them with the peanut butter frosting using a piping bag or an offset spatula.

Optional Garnish:
- Garnish with chopped peanuts or mini chocolate chips if desired.

Enjoy:
- Your Peanut Butter Cupcakes are ready to be enjoyed!

These cupcakes are a delightful treat for peanut butter lovers, combining a moist and flavorful cake with a creamy peanut butter frosting.

Peanut Butter Granola Bars

Ingredients:

- 2 cups old-fashioned oats
- 1 cup crispy rice cereal
- 1/2 cup honey or maple syrup
- 1/2 cup creamy peanut butter
- 1 teaspoon vanilla extract
- 1/2 cup chopped nuts (e.g., almonds, peanuts) - optional
- 1/4 cup mini chocolate chips - optional

Instructions:

Prepare Pan:
- Line a 9x9-inch (23x23 cm) square baking pan with parchment paper, leaving an overhang on the sides for easy removal.

Combine Dry Ingredients:
- In a large bowl, combine the old-fashioned oats and crispy rice cereal. If using, add chopped nuts and mini chocolate chips.

Heat Peanut Butter and Honey:
- In a small saucepan over low heat, warm the peanut butter and honey (or maple syrup), stirring until well combined. Remove from heat and stir in the vanilla extract.

Combine Wet and Dry Ingredients:
- Pour the warm peanut butter mixture over the dry ingredients. Stir well until everything is evenly coated.

Press into Pan:
- Transfer the mixture to the prepared baking pan. Press it down firmly and evenly using a spatula or the back of a spoon.

Chill:
- Place the pan in the refrigerator and let it chill for at least 2 hours or until the granola bars are firm.

Cut into Bars:
- Once chilled, lift the granola slab out of the pan using the parchment paper overhang. Place it on a cutting board and cut it into bars.

Store:

- Store the Peanut Butter Granola Bars in an airtight container in the refrigerator for freshness. They can also be individually wrapped for on-the-go snacks.

Enjoy:
- Enjoy these homemade Peanut Butter Granola Bars as a delicious and satisfying snack!

Feel free to customize these granola bars by adding dried fruit, seeds, or your favorite mix-ins. They are a healthier alternative to store-bought bars and can be tailored to suit your taste preferences.

Peanut Butter and Banana Bread

Ingredients:

- 3 ripe bananas, mashed
- 1/2 cup creamy peanut butter
- 1/4 cup unsalted butter, melted
- 1/2 cup granulated sugar
- 1/2 cup brown sugar, packed
- 1 large egg
- 1 teaspoon vanilla extract
- 1 1/2 cups all-purpose flour
- 1 teaspoon baking soda
- 1/2 teaspoon baking powder
- 1/4 teaspoon salt
- 1/2 cup milk (dairy or plant-based)
- Optional: 1/2 cup chopped nuts (e.g., walnuts or pecans)

Instructions:

Preheat Oven:
- Preheat your oven to 350°F (175°C). Grease and flour a 9x5-inch (23x13 cm) loaf pan.

Mash Bananas:
- In a large mixing bowl, mash the ripe bananas with a fork.

Combine Wet Ingredients:
- Add creamy peanut butter, melted butter, granulated sugar, brown sugar, egg, and vanilla extract to the mashed bananas. Mix until well combined.

Combine Dry Ingredients:
- In a separate bowl, whisk together the all-purpose flour, baking soda, baking powder, and salt.

Add Dry Ingredients to Wet Ingredients:
- Gradually add the dry ingredients to the wet ingredients, mixing until just combined.

Add Milk and Nuts:
- Pour in the milk and stir until smooth. If using, fold in the chopped nuts.

Pour into Pan:
- Pour the batter into the prepared loaf pan, spreading it evenly.

Bake:
- Bake in the preheated oven for 60-70 minutes or until a toothpick inserted into the center comes out clean.

Cool:
- Allow the Peanut Butter and Banana Bread to cool in the pan for 10 minutes, then transfer it to a wire rack to cool completely.

Slice and Serve:
- Once cooled, slice the bread and serve. Enjoy it as is or with a spread of peanut butter for an extra treat!

This Peanut Butter and Banana Bread is moist, flavorful, and the combination of peanut butter and bananas is a delightful twist on the classic banana bread.

Peanut Butter Hummus

Ingredients:

- 1 can (15 ounces) chickpeas, drained and rinsed
- 1/4 cup creamy peanut butter
- 1/4 cup olive oil
- 2 tablespoons tahini
- 2 cloves garlic, minced
- 1 lemon, juiced
- 1/2 teaspoon ground cumin
- Salt and pepper to taste
- Water (as needed for desired consistency)
- Optional garnishes: drizzle of olive oil, chopped peanuts, or chopped fresh parsley

Instructions:

Prepare Chickpeas:
- Rinse and drain the chickpeas thoroughly.

Combine Ingredients:
- In a food processor, combine the chickpeas, peanut butter, olive oil, tahini, minced garlic, lemon juice, ground cumin, salt, and pepper.

Blend Until Smooth:
- Blend the ingredients until smooth. If the mixture is too thick, you can add water, one tablespoon at a time, until you reach your desired consistency.

Adjust Seasonings:
- Taste the hummus and adjust the seasonings, adding more salt, pepper, or lemon juice as needed.

Serve:
- Transfer the Peanut Butter Hummus to a serving bowl.

Garnish (Optional):
- Drizzle with olive oil and garnish with chopped peanuts or fresh parsley.

Serve and Enjoy:
- Serve the Peanut Butter Hummus with pita bread, vegetable sticks, or crackers. It can also be used as a spread or dip for various snacks.

This unique hummus recipe adds a nutty and creamy flavor to the classic chickpea dip. It's a perfect appetizer or snack for those who love the combination of peanut butter and savory flavors.

Peanut Butter Chocolate Milkshake

Ingredients:

- 2 cups chocolate ice cream
- 1/2 cup milk (dairy or plant-based)
- 2 tablespoons creamy peanut butter
- 2 tablespoons chocolate syrup
- Whipped cream for topping (optional)
- Chopped peanuts for garnish (optional)

Instructions:

Prepare Ingredients:
- Allow the chocolate ice cream to soften slightly before using.

Blend Ingredients:
- In a blender, combine the softened chocolate ice cream, milk, creamy peanut butter, and chocolate syrup.

Blend Until Smooth:
- Blend the ingredients until smooth and well combined. If the milkshake is too thick, you can add more milk, a little at a time, until you reach your desired consistency.

Check Consistency:
- Taste the milkshake and adjust the sweetness or thickness by adding more chocolate syrup or milk if needed.

Pour into Glasses:
- Pour the Peanut Butter Chocolate Milkshake into glasses.

Top with Whipped Cream (Optional):
- If desired, top the milkshake with a generous dollop of whipped cream.

Garnish (Optional):
- Sprinkle chopped peanuts on top for an extra crunch and visual appeal.

Serve and Enjoy:
- Serve the Peanut Butter Chocolate Milkshake immediately and enjoy this deliciously indulgent treat!

This milkshake combines the rich flavors of chocolate and peanut butter for a satisfying and decadent beverage. It's perfect for a sweet treat on a warm day or as a delightful dessert.

Peanut Butter Oatmeal Cookies

Ingredients:

- 1 cup unsalted butter, softened
- 1 cup creamy peanut butter
- 1 cup granulated sugar
- 1 cup packed brown sugar
- 2 large eggs
- 1 teaspoon vanilla extract
- 2 cups old-fashioned oats
- 2 cups all-purpose flour
- 1 teaspoon baking soda
- 1/2 teaspoon baking powder
- 1/2 teaspoon salt

Instructions:

Preheat Oven:
- Preheat your oven to 350°F (175°C). Line baking sheets with parchment paper.

Cream Butter, Peanut Butter, and Sugars:
- In a large bowl, cream together softened butter, creamy peanut butter, granulated sugar, and brown sugar until smooth and fluffy.

Add Eggs and Vanilla:
- Add the eggs one at a time, beating well after each addition. Stir in the vanilla extract.

Combine Dry Ingredients:
- In a separate bowl, whisk together oats, all-purpose flour, baking soda, baking powder, and salt.

Mix Wet and Dry Ingredients:
- Gradually add the dry ingredients to the peanut butter mixture, mixing until just combined. Do not overmix.

Form Dough:
- Drop rounded tablespoons of dough onto the prepared baking sheets, leaving some space between each cookie.

Flatten with Fork (Optional):

- Optionally, you can flatten each cookie with a fork, creating a crisscross pattern on top.

Bake:
- Bake in the preheated oven for 10-12 minutes or until the edges are golden brown.

Cool:
- Allow the cookies to cool on the baking sheets for a few minutes before transferring them to a wire rack to cool completely.

Enjoy:
- Once cooled, enjoy these Peanut Butter Oatmeal Cookies with a glass of milk or your favorite beverage!

These cookies are a delightful combination of the nutty flavor of peanut butter and the chewiness of oats. They make for a perfect treat for peanut butter lovers!

Peanut Butter and Jelly Thumbprint Cookies

Ingredients:

- 1 cup unsalted butter, softened
- 3/4 cup creamy peanut butter
- 1 cup granulated sugar
- 1 large egg
- 1 teaspoon vanilla extract
- 2 1/2 cups all-purpose flour
- 1/2 teaspoon baking powder
- 1/2 teaspoon salt
- Your favorite fruit jam or jelly for filling

Instructions:

Preheat Oven:
- Preheat your oven to 350°F (175°C). Line baking sheets with parchment paper.

Cream Butter, Peanut Butter, and Sugar:
- In a large bowl, cream together softened butter, creamy peanut butter, and granulated sugar until light and fluffy.

Add Egg and Vanilla:
- Beat in the egg and vanilla extract until well combined.

Combine Dry Ingredients:
- In a separate bowl, whisk together all-purpose flour, baking powder, and salt.

Mix Wet and Dry Ingredients:
- Gradually add the dry ingredients to the peanut butter mixture, mixing until just combined. Do not overmix.

Form Cookie Dough Balls:
- Scoop tablespoon-sized portions of dough and roll them into balls. Place them on the prepared baking sheets, leaving some space between each.

Make Thumbprint Indentation:
- Use your thumb or the back of a spoon to make an indentation in the center of each cookie.

Fill with Jam:

- Spoon a small amount of your favorite fruit jam or jelly into the indentation of each cookie.

Bake:
- Bake in the preheated oven for 10-12 minutes or until the edges are golden brown.

Cool:
- Allow the cookies to cool on the baking sheets for a few minutes before transferring them to a wire rack to cool completely.

Enjoy:
- Once cooled, enjoy these delightful Peanut Butter and Jelly Thumbprint Cookies!

These cookies are a nostalgic and comforting treat, combining the classic flavors of peanut butter and jelly in a delightful thumbprint cookie.

Peanut Butter Swirl Brownies

Ingredients:

For the Brownie Batter:

- 1 cup unsalted butter, melted
- 2 cups granulated sugar
- 1 cup all-purpose flour
- 1 cup cocoa powder
- 1/2 teaspoon baking powder
- 1/4 teaspoon salt
- 4 large eggs
- 2 teaspoons vanilla extract

For the Peanut Butter Swirl:

- 1 cup creamy peanut butter
- 1/2 cup powdered sugar
- 1/4 cup unsalted butter, softened
- 1 teaspoon vanilla extract

Instructions:

Preheat Oven:
- Preheat your oven to 350°F (175°C). Grease and line a 9x13-inch (23x33 cm) baking pan with parchment paper.

Prepare Brownie Batter:
- In a large mixing bowl, whisk together the melted butter and granulated sugar until well combined.

Add Dry Ingredients:
- Sift in the all-purpose flour, cocoa powder, baking powder, and salt. Mix until the dry ingredients are fully incorporated into the wet mixture.

Add Eggs and Vanilla:
- Add the eggs one at a time, mixing well after each addition. Stir in the vanilla extract.

Prepare Peanut Butter Swirl:
- In a separate bowl, mix together the creamy peanut butter, powdered sugar, softened butter, and vanilla extract until smooth.

Layer Batter and Peanut Butter Swirl:
- Pour about two-thirds of the brownie batter into the prepared baking pan. Drop spoonfuls of the peanut butter swirl mixture on top. Using a knife or spatula, gently swirl the peanut butter into the brownie batter.

Top with Remaining Batter:
- Pour the remaining brownie batter over the peanut butter swirl layer.

Swirl Again:
- Create more swirls by gently running a knife through the top layer of brownie batter and peanut butter.

Bake:
- Bake in the preheated oven for 30-35 minutes or until a toothpick inserted into the center comes out with a few moist crumbs.

Cool and Slice:
- Allow the brownies to cool completely in the pan before slicing into squares.

Enjoy:
- Enjoy these Peanut Butter Swirl Brownies as a delightful and decadent treat!

These brownies combine the rich flavors of chocolate and peanut butter for a mouthwatering dessert that's sure to satisfy your sweet cravings.

Peanut Butter Cheesecake

Ingredients:

For the Crust:

- 2 cups graham cracker crumbs
- 1/2 cup unsalted butter, melted
- 1/4 cup granulated sugar

For the Cheesecake Filling:

- 4 packages (8 ounces each) cream cheese, softened
- 1 and 1/2 cups granulated sugar
- 1 cup creamy peanut butter
- 4 large eggs
- 1 teaspoon vanilla extract
- 1 cup sour cream

For the Peanut Butter Ganache:

- 1/2 cup heavy cream
- 1 cup semi-sweet chocolate chips
- 1/2 cup creamy peanut butter

Instructions:

Preheat Oven:
- Preheat your oven to 325°F (163°C). Grease a 9-inch (23 cm) springform pan.

Make the Crust:
- In a bowl, combine graham cracker crumbs, melted butter, and granulated sugar. Press the mixture into the bottom of the prepared springform pan to form the crust.

Prepare Cheesecake Filling:

- In a large mixing bowl, beat the softened cream cheese and granulated sugar until smooth and creamy. Add peanut butter and continue to beat until well combined.

Add Eggs and Vanilla:
- Add eggs one at a time, beating well after each addition. Stir in the vanilla extract.

Incorporate Sour Cream:
- Mix in the sour cream until the batter is smooth and well combined.

Pour into Crust:
- Pour the cheesecake filling over the crust in the springform pan, spreading it evenly.

Bake:
- Bake in the preheated oven for about 55-60 minutes or until the center is set and the top is lightly browned.

Cool:
- Allow the cheesecake to cool in the pan on a wire rack for about 10 minutes. Run a knife around the edge to loosen the cheesecake from the sides of the pan.

Prepare Peanut Butter Ganache:
- In a small saucepan, heat the heavy cream until it simmers. Remove from heat and stir in chocolate chips and peanut butter until smooth.

Pour Ganache Over Cheesecake:
- Pour the peanut butter ganache over the cooled cheesecake, spreading it evenly.

Chill:
- Refrigerate the cheesecake for at least 4 hours, or preferably overnight, to allow it to set.

Serve:
- Once fully chilled and set, remove the cheesecake from the springform pan, slice, and serve.

Enjoy:
- Enjoy this decadent Peanut Butter Cheesecake as a delightful dessert!

This Peanut Butter Cheesecake is rich, creamy, and perfect for those who love the combination of peanut butter and cheesecake.

Peanut Butter Banana Muffins

Ingredients:

- 1 and 1/2 cups ripe bananas, mashed (about 3-4 bananas)
- 1/2 cup creamy peanut butter
- 1/4 cup unsalted butter, melted
- 1/2 cup granulated sugar
- 1/2 cup brown sugar, packed
- 1 large egg
- 1 teaspoon vanilla extract
- 1 and 1/2 cups all-purpose flour
- 1 teaspoon baking soda
- 1/2 teaspoon baking powder
- 1/4 teaspoon salt
- 1/2 cup milk (dairy or plant-based)
- Optional: 1/2 cup chopped nuts or chocolate chips

Instructions:

Preheat Oven:
- Preheat your oven to 350°F (175°C). Line a muffin tin with paper liners or grease the cups.

Mash Bananas:
- In a bowl, mash the ripe bananas with a fork until smooth.

Combine Wet Ingredients:
- In a large mixing bowl, combine the mashed bananas, creamy peanut butter, melted butter, granulated sugar, brown sugar, egg, and vanilla extract. Mix until well combined.

Add Dry Ingredients:
- In a separate bowl, whisk together the all-purpose flour, baking soda, baking powder, and salt.

Combine Wet and Dry Ingredients:
- Gradually add the dry ingredients to the wet ingredients, mixing until just combined. Do not overmix.

Add Milk:
- Pour in the milk and stir until the batter is smooth.

Optional Add-ins:

- If desired, fold in chopped nuts or chocolate chips into the batter.

Fill Muffin Cups:
- Spoon the batter into the prepared muffin cups, filling each about 2/3 full.

Bake:
- Bake in the preheated oven for 18-20 minutes or until a toothpick inserted into the center comes out clean.

Cool:
- Allow the muffins to cool in the tin for a few minutes before transferring them to a wire rack to cool completely.

Serve and Enjoy:
- Once cooled, these Peanut Butter Banana Muffins are ready to be enjoyed!

These muffins are a delightful blend of sweet bananas and creamy peanut butter, making them a perfect breakfast or snack option.

Peanut Butter Ice Cream

Ingredients:

- 2 cups heavy cream
- 1 cup whole milk
- 3/4 cup granulated sugar
- 1/2 cup creamy peanut butter
- 1 teaspoon vanilla extract
- 1/2 cup chopped peanuts (optional, for added texture)

Instructions:

Prepare Ice Cream Base:
- In a mixing bowl, whisk together heavy cream, whole milk, and granulated sugar until the sugar is dissolved.

Melt Peanut Butter:
- In a separate microwave-safe bowl, heat the creamy peanut butter until it becomes smooth and pourable. You can do this in short 15-20 second bursts, stirring in between.

Combine Peanut Butter with Ice Cream Base:
- Whisk the melted peanut butter into the ice cream base until well combined.

Add Vanilla Extract:
- Stir in the vanilla extract, ensuring it is evenly distributed.

Chill the Mixture:
- Cover the bowl and refrigerate the mixture for at least 4 hours or overnight. This allows the flavors to meld and the mixture to chill thoroughly.

Freeze in Ice Cream Maker:
- Pour the chilled mixture into an ice cream maker and churn according to the manufacturer's instructions. This usually takes about 20-25 minutes.

Optional: Add Chopped Peanuts:
- If you like, add chopped peanuts during the last few minutes of churning for added texture.

Transfer to Container:
- Transfer the churned ice cream to a lidded container, spreading it evenly.

Freeze:

- Freeze the ice cream for at least 4 hours or until it reaches your desired consistency.

Serve and Enjoy:
- Scoop the Peanut Butter Ice Cream into bowls or cones and enjoy!

This homemade Peanut Butter Ice Cream is rich, creamy, and has a wonderful peanut butter flavor. Feel free to customize it by adding in chocolate chips, swirls of chocolate sauce, or your favorite mix-ins!

Peanut Butter Pretzel Bites

Ingredients:

- 1 cup creamy peanut butter
- 1/4 cup unsalted butter, softened
- 2 cups powdered sugar
- Pretzel twists (mini or regular-sized)
- 10 ounces chocolate chips (semi-sweet or milk chocolate)
- 1 tablespoon vegetable shortening (optional, for smoother chocolate coating)

Instructions:

Prepare Peanut Butter Filling:
- In a mixing bowl, combine creamy peanut butter, softened butter, and powdered sugar. Mix until well combined and smooth.

Form Peanut Butter Balls:
- Take small portions of the peanut butter mixture and roll them into small balls. The size of the balls will depend on your preference.

Assemble Peanut Butter Pretzel Bites:
- Sandwich each peanut butter ball between two pretzel twists, pressing gently to adhere.

Prepare Chocolate Coating:
- In a microwave-safe bowl or using a double boiler, melt the chocolate chips. If desired, add vegetable shortening to the melted chocolate for a smoother coating.

Coat Pretzel Bites in Chocolate:
- Dip each assembled peanut butter pretzel bite into the melted chocolate, ensuring it is fully coated. Use a fork to lift it out, allowing excess chocolate to drip off.

Place on Parchment Paper:
- Place the coated pretzel bites on a parchment paper-lined tray.

Chill:
- Refrigerate the peanut butter pretzel bites for about 30 minutes or until the chocolate coating is set.

Serve and Enjoy:
- Once set, these Peanut Butter Pretzel Bites are ready to be enjoyed! Store any leftovers in an airtight container.

These sweet and salty treats are perfect for satisfying your peanut butter and chocolate cravings. They make for a great snack or a delightful addition to parties and gatherings.

Peanut Butter Cup Smoothie Bowl

Ingredients:

For the Smoothie Base:

- 2 frozen bananas, sliced
- 1/2 cup Greek yogurt
- 1/4 cup creamy peanut butter
- 1 tablespoon cocoa powder
- 1/2 cup milk (dairy or plant-based)
- 1 teaspoon honey or maple syrup (optional, depending on sweetness preference)
- Ice cubes (optional, for a thicker consistency)

For Toppings:

- Chopped peanuts
- Dark chocolate chips or chunks
- Sliced bananas
- Drizzle of peanut butter
- Granola

Instructions:

Prepare Smoothie Base:
- In a blender, combine frozen banana slices, Greek yogurt, creamy peanut butter, cocoa powder, milk, and honey or maple syrup. If you prefer a thicker consistency, you can add a handful of ice cubes.

Blend Until Smooth:
- Blend the ingredients until smooth and creamy. You may need to stop and scrape down the sides of the blender to ensure all ingredients are well incorporated.

Adjust Consistency:
- If the smoothie is too thick, add a little more milk. If it's too thin, add more frozen banana slices or ice cubes.

Pour into Bowl:
- Pour the smoothie into a bowl.

Add Toppings:

- Top the smoothie bowl with chopped peanuts, dark chocolate chips or chunks, sliced bananas, a drizzle of peanut butter, and granola.

Create a Swirl (Optional):
- For a decorative touch, you can use a toothpick or a knife to create a swirl with the peanut butter on top of the smoothie bowl.

Enjoy:
- Enjoy your Peanut Butter Cup Smoothie Bowl immediately with a spoon!

This smoothie bowl combines the classic flavors of peanut butter and chocolate in a nutritious and satisfying breakfast or snack. Customize the toppings based on your preferences for a delightful treat.

Peanut Butter and Chocolate Tart

Ingredients:

For the Crust:

- 1 and 1/2 cups chocolate cookie crumbs (about 20 chocolate sandwich cookies)
- 1/3 cup unsalted butter, melted

For the Peanut Butter Filling:

- 1 cup creamy peanut butter
- 1/2 cup powdered sugar
- 1/4 cup unsalted butter, softened
- 1 teaspoon vanilla extract

For the Chocolate Ganache:

- 1 cup semi-sweet chocolate chips
- 1/2 cup heavy cream

For Garnish (Optional):

- Chopped peanuts
- Chocolate shavings

Instructions:

Prepare the Crust:
- In a food processor, pulse the chocolate sandwich cookies until they become fine crumbs. Mix the crumbs with melted butter until well combined. Press the mixture into the bottom and up the sides of a tart pan. Refrigerate the crust while preparing the filling.

Make the Peanut Butter Filling:
- In a bowl, beat together creamy peanut butter, powdered sugar, softened butter, and vanilla extract until smooth and well combined.

Fill the Crust:
- Spread the peanut butter filling evenly over the chilled crust. Smooth the top with a spatula.

Prepare Chocolate Ganache:

- In a small saucepan, heat the heavy cream until it simmers. Remove from heat and pour over the chocolate chips in a heatproof bowl. Let it sit for a minute, then stir until smooth.

Pour Ganache Over Peanut Butter Filling:
- Pour the chocolate ganache over the peanut butter filling, spreading it evenly.

Chill:
- Refrigerate the tart for at least 2-3 hours, or until it is set.

Garnish (Optional):
- Before serving, garnish the tart with chopped peanuts and chocolate shavings if desired.

Slice and Serve:
- Once set, slice and serve this indulgent Peanut Butter and Chocolate Tart.

This tart combines the irresistible flavors of peanut butter and chocolate in a rich and satisfying dessert. It's a perfect treat for peanut butter and chocolate lovers!

Peanut Butter and Honey Toast

Ingredients:

- Slices of your favorite bread (whole wheat, sourdough, or any preferred type)
- Creamy peanut butter
- Honey

Instructions:

Toast the Bread:
- Toast the slices of bread to your desired level of doneness.

Spread Peanut Butter:
- While the toast is still warm, spread a generous layer of creamy peanut butter evenly on each slice.

Drizzle with Honey:
- Drizzle honey over the peanut butter. The amount of honey can be adjusted based on your sweetness preference.

Optional Additions:
- Optionally, you can add a sprinkle of cinnamon, sliced bananas, or a dash of chia seeds for extra flavor and texture.

Serve and Enjoy:
- Serve the Peanut Butter and Honey Toast immediately and enjoy this quick and tasty snack or breakfast.

This combination of peanut butter and honey offers a delightful blend of nutty, creamy, and sweet flavors. It's a classic and satisfying choice for a quick and nutritious bite.

Peanut Butter Cup Cookies

Ingredients:

- 1 and 3/4 cups all-purpose flour
- 1/2 teaspoon baking soda
- 1/2 teaspoon salt
- 1/2 cup unsalted butter, softened
- 1/2 cup granulated sugar
- 1/2 cup packed brown sugar
- 1/2 cup creamy peanut butter
- 1 large egg
- 1 teaspoon vanilla extract
- Mini peanut butter cups, unwrapped

Instructions:

Preheat Oven:
- Preheat your oven to 350°F (175°C). Line baking sheets with parchment paper.

Combine Dry Ingredients:
- In a medium bowl, whisk together the all-purpose flour, baking soda, and salt. Set aside.

Cream Butter and Sugars:
- In a large bowl, cream together the softened butter, granulated sugar, and brown sugar until light and fluffy.

Add Peanut Butter, Egg, and Vanilla:
- Add the creamy peanut butter, egg, and vanilla extract to the creamed butter and sugar. Mix until well combined.

Incorporate Dry Ingredients:
- Gradually add the dry ingredients to the wet ingredients, mixing until just combined. Do not overmix.

Form Cookie Dough Balls:
- Scoop out tablespoon-sized portions of dough and roll them into balls. Place the cookie dough balls on the prepared baking sheets, leaving space between each.

Press Peanut Butter Cups:
- Press a mini peanut butter cup into the center of each cookie dough ball, slightly flattening the cookies.

Bake:
- Bake in the preheated oven for 10-12 minutes or until the edges are golden brown.

Cool on Baking Sheets:
- Allow the cookies to cool on the baking sheets for a few minutes before transferring them to a wire rack to cool completely.

Enjoy:
- Once cooled, enjoy these Peanut Butter Cup Cookies with a glass of milk or your favorite beverage!

These cookies are a delightful combination of soft and chewy peanut butter cookie dough with a gooey peanut butter cup in the center. They are perfect for peanut butter lovers and make for a delicious treat.

Peanut Butter Protein Balls

Ingredients:

- 1 cup old-fashioned oats
- 1/2 cup creamy peanut butter
- 1/3 cup honey or maple syrup
- 1/2 cup protein powder (whey, pea, or your preferred type)
- 1/2 cup ground flaxseed or chia seeds
- 1 teaspoon vanilla extract
- A pinch of salt (optional)
- Optional add-ins: dark chocolate chips, chopped nuts, or dried fruit

Instructions:

Combine Dry Ingredients:
- In a large bowl, combine the old-fashioned oats, protein powder, and ground flaxseed or chia seeds.

Add Wet Ingredients:
- Add the creamy peanut butter, honey or maple syrup, vanilla extract, and a pinch of salt (if using) to the dry ingredients.

Mix Well:
- Mix the ingredients thoroughly until well combined. The mixture should be sticky and hold together.

Optional Add-ins:
- If desired, fold in dark chocolate chips, chopped nuts, or dried fruit for added texture and flavor.

Chill the Mixture:
- Place the mixture in the refrigerator for about 30 minutes. Chilling makes it easier to handle and shape into balls.

Shape into Balls:
- Once chilled, take small portions of the mixture and roll them into bite-sized balls.

Store:
- Store the Peanut Butter Protein Balls in an airtight container in the refrigerator for freshness. They can also be frozen for longer storage.

Enjoy:
- Enjoy these protein-packed snacks as a quick and nutritious pick-me-up during the day or before a workout.

These Peanut Butter Protein Balls are not only tasty but also provide a good balance of protein, healthy fats, and fiber, making them a great snack for sustained energy.

Thai Peanut Chicken Satay

Ingredients:

For the Chicken Marinade:

- 1.5 lbs (700g) boneless, skinless chicken thighs or breasts, cut into strips

For the Marinade:

- 1/4 cup soy sauce
- 3 tablespoons fish sauce
- 2 tablespoons lime juice
- 2 tablespoons honey
- 2 tablespoons peanut butter
- 2 cloves garlic, minced
- 1 teaspoon ground coriander
- 1 teaspoon ground cumin
- 1 teaspoon turmeric powder
- 1 teaspoon paprika

For the Peanut Sauce:

- 1/2 cup peanut butter
- 1/4 cup soy sauce
- 2 tablespoons lime juice
- 1 tablespoon honey
- 1 teaspoon grated ginger
- 1 clove garlic, minced
- 1/4 cup coconut milk (or more for desired consistency)

For Serving:

- Chopped cilantro for garnish
- Crushed peanuts for garnish
- Lime wedges

Instructions:

Prepare Marinade:

- In a bowl, whisk together all the marinade ingredients until well combined.

Marinate Chicken:
- Place the chicken strips in a zip-top bag or shallow dish and pour the marinade over them. Seal the bag or cover the dish and refrigerate for at least 1-2 hours, or ideally overnight.

Prepare Peanut Sauce:
- In a small saucepan, combine all the peanut sauce ingredients over low heat. Stir continuously until the peanut butter is melted and the sauce is smooth. If needed, add more coconut milk for your desired consistency. Set aside.

Thread Chicken onto Skewers:
- Preheat the grill or grill pan. Thread the marinated chicken strips onto skewers.

Grill Chicken:
- Grill the chicken skewers for 4-5 minutes per side or until cooked through and slightly charred.

Serve:
- Arrange the grilled chicken skewers on a serving platter. Drizzle with some of the peanut sauce and garnish with chopped cilantro and crushed peanuts. Serve with lime wedges on the side.

Enjoy:
- Serve the Thai Peanut Chicken Satay with extra peanut sauce on the side for dipping. Enjoy!

This Thai Peanut Chicken Satay is flavorful, tender, and perfect for a delicious appetizer or main dish. The peanut sauce adds a rich and creamy element to the grilled chicken.

Peanut Butter Cup Cheesecake Bars

Ingredients:

For the Crust:

- 1 and 1/2 cups graham cracker crumbs
- 1/2 cup unsalted butter, melted
- 1/4 cup granulated sugar

For the Cheesecake Filling:

- 3 packages (24 ounces) cream cheese, softened
- 1 cup granulated sugar
- 3 large eggs
- 1 teaspoon vanilla extract
- 1/2 cup creamy peanut butter
- 1/2 cup sour cream

For Topping:

- Mini peanut butter cups, halved
- Chocolate ganache (optional)

Instructions:

Preheat Oven:
- Preheat your oven to 325°F (163°C). Line a 9x13-inch baking pan with parchment paper, leaving some overhang for easy removal.

Make the Crust:
- In a bowl, combine graham cracker crumbs, melted butter, and granulated sugar. Press the mixture into the bottom of the prepared pan to form the crust.

Bake the Crust:
- Bake the crust in the preheated oven for about 8-10 minutes or until lightly golden. Remove from the oven and allow it to cool while preparing the filling.

Prepare Cheesecake Filling:
- In a large mixing bowl, beat the softened cream cheese until smooth. Add granulated sugar and continue to beat until well combined.

Add Eggs and Vanilla:
- Add eggs one at a time, beating well after each addition. Stir in the vanilla extract.

Incorporate Peanut Butter and Sour Cream:
- Add creamy peanut butter and sour cream to the cream cheese mixture. Mix until smooth and creamy.

Pour Over Crust:
- Pour the cheesecake filling over the cooled crust, spreading it evenly.

Bake Cheesecake:
- Bake in the preheated oven for about 35-40 minutes or until the center is set. The edges should be slightly golden.

Cool and Chill:
- Allow the cheesecake to cool in the pan, then refrigerate for at least 4 hours or overnight.

Top with Peanut Butter Cups:
- Once chilled, top the cheesecake with halved mini peanut butter cups.

Optional: Add Chocolate Ganache:
- If desired, drizzle chocolate ganache over the top for an extra layer of indulgence.

Slice and Serve:
- Use the parchment paper overhang to lift the cheesecake out of the pan. Slice into bars and serve.

Enjoy:
- Enjoy these Peanut Butter Cup Cheesecake Bars as a decadent and delightful dessert!

These bars combine the creamy richness of cheesecake with the irresistible flavors of peanut butter and chocolate. Perfect for satisfying your sweet cravings!

Peanut Butter and Chocolate Truffles

Ingredients:

For the Truffle Filling:

- 1 cup creamy peanut butter
- 1/4 cup unsalted butter, softened
- 2 cups powdered sugar
- 1 teaspoon vanilla extract

For the Chocolate Coating:

- 12 ounces (about 2 cups) semisweet or milk chocolate chips
- 2 tablespoons unsalted butter

Optional Toppings:

- Crushed peanuts
- Cocoa powder
- Finely chopped nuts

Instructions:

Prepare Truffle Filling:
- In a bowl, combine creamy peanut butter, softened butter, powdered sugar, and vanilla extract. Mix until well combined and smooth.

Form Truffle Balls:
- Scoop out small portions of the peanut butter mixture and roll them into bite-sized balls. Place the balls on a parchment-lined tray.

Chill Truffles:
- Place the tray in the refrigerator and chill the peanut butter truffle balls for at least 30 minutes to firm them up.

Prepare Chocolate Coating:
- In a microwave-safe bowl or using a double boiler, melt the chocolate chips and unsalted butter together. Stir until smooth.

Coat Truffles in Chocolate:

- Using a fork or toothpick, dip each chilled peanut butter truffle into the melted chocolate, ensuring it is fully coated. Allow excess chocolate to drip off.

Place on Tray:
- Place the coated truffles back on the parchment-lined tray.

Add Toppings (Optional):
- While the chocolate coating is still wet, you can sprinkle crushed peanuts, cocoa powder, or finely chopped nuts on top for added texture and flavor.

Chill Again:
- Place the tray back in the refrigerator to allow the chocolate coating to set completely. This typically takes about 1-2 hours.

Serve and Enjoy:
- Once the chocolate is set, your Peanut Butter and Chocolate Truffles are ready to be enjoyed. Store any leftovers in the refrigerator.

These truffles are a perfect combination of rich peanut butter and smooth chocolate, making them a delightful treat for any occasion.

Peanut Butter Banana Bread Pudding

Ingredients:

- 4 cups day-old bread (such as French bread or brioche), cubed
- 2 ripe bananas, mashed
- 1/2 cup creamy peanut butter
- 2 cups milk (whole or any preferred type)
- 1/2 cup heavy cream
- 3/4 cup granulated sugar
- 4 large eggs
- 1 teaspoon vanilla extract
- 1/2 teaspoon ground cinnamon
- 1/4 teaspoon salt
- 1/2 cup chocolate chips (optional)
- Chopped peanuts for garnish (optional)

Instructions:

Preheat Oven:
- Preheat your oven to 350°F (175°C). Grease a baking dish.

Prepare Bread Cubes:
- Cut the day-old bread into cubes and place them in the greased baking dish.

Make Peanut Butter Banana Mixture:
- In a bowl, combine mashed bananas and creamy peanut butter. Mix until well combined.

Layer Bread and Peanut Butter Banana Mixture:
- Spread the peanut butter banana mixture over the bread cubes in the baking dish.

Prepare Custard Mixture:
- In another bowl, whisk together milk, heavy cream, granulated sugar, eggs, vanilla extract, ground cinnamon, and salt until well combined.

Pour Custard Over Bread:
- Pour the custard mixture over the bread and banana mixture in the baking dish. Press down slightly to ensure the bread cubes absorb the liquid.

Add Chocolate Chips (Optional):
- If using chocolate chips, sprinkle them over the top of the bread pudding.

Bake:

- Bake in the preheated oven for 45-50 minutes or until the top is golden brown and the custard is set.

Cool:
- Allow the peanut butter banana bread pudding to cool for a few minutes before serving.

Garnish and Serve:
- Garnish with chopped peanuts if desired. Serve warm and enjoy!

This Peanut Butter Banana Bread Pudding is a comforting and flavorful dessert, perfect for using up ripe bananas and creating a delightful treat.

Peanut Butter and Chocolate Pretzel Bark

Ingredients:

- 2 cups pretzels, broken into pieces
- 1 cup creamy peanut butter
- 12 ounces (about 2 cups) semisweet or milk chocolate chips
- 1/2 cup white chocolate chips (optional, for drizzling)

Instructions:

Prepare Baking Sheet:
- Line a baking sheet with parchment paper.

Spread Pretzels:
- Spread the broken pretzel pieces evenly on the parchment paper, creating a single layer.

Melt Peanut Butter:
- In a microwave-safe bowl, heat the creamy peanut butter until it becomes smooth and pourable. This usually takes about 20-30 seconds in the microwave.

Drizzle Peanut Butter Over Pretzels:
- Drizzle the melted peanut butter evenly over the pretzel pieces.

Melt Chocolate:
- In another microwave-safe bowl, melt the chocolate chips in 20-30 second intervals, stirring between each interval until the chocolate is fully melted.

Spread Chocolate Over Peanut Butter and Pretzels:
- Pour the melted chocolate over the peanut butter and pretzels, spreading it evenly with a spatula.

Optional: Melt White Chocolate for Drizzle:
- If using white chocolate for drizzling, melt it in the microwave in 20-30 second intervals until smooth.

Drizzle White Chocolate (Optional):
- Drizzle the melted white chocolate over the dark chocolate layer using a spoon or a piping bag.

Chill:
- Place the baking sheet in the refrigerator for at least 1-2 hours or until the bark is fully set.

Break into Pieces:
- Once set, break the Peanut Butter and Chocolate Pretzel Bark into pieces.

Serve and Enjoy:
- Serve and enjoy this sweet and salty treat!

This Peanut Butter and Chocolate Pretzel Bark is a delightful combination of crunchy pretzels, creamy peanut butter, and rich chocolate. It makes for a great homemade snack or gift.

Peanut Butter Rice Krispie Treats

Ingredients:

- 6 cups Rice Krispies cereal
- 1/2 cup unsalted butter
- 1 cup creamy peanut butter
- 1 package (10 ounces) marshmallows
- 1 teaspoon vanilla extract
- Pinch of salt (optional)

Instructions:

Prepare Baking Dish:
- Grease a 9x13-inch baking dish or line it with parchment paper.

Melt Butter and Peanut Butter:
- In a large pot over low heat, melt the butter and peanut butter together, stirring until smooth.

Add Marshmallows:
- Add the marshmallows to the melted butter and peanut butter mixture. Stir continuously until the marshmallows are completely melted and the mixture is smooth.

Remove from Heat:
- Remove the pot from heat and stir in the vanilla extract. If desired, add a pinch of salt for balance.

Add Rice Krispies:
- Add the Rice Krispies cereal to the pot, stirring until the cereal is well coated with the peanut butter and marshmallow mixture.

Press into Baking Dish:
- Transfer the mixture to the prepared baking dish. Use a spatula or wax paper to press it evenly into the dish.

Cool:
- Allow the Peanut Butter Rice Krispie Treats to cool and set for at least 1-2 hours.

Cut into Squares:
- Once the treats have fully set, cut them into squares or rectangles.

Serve and Enjoy:
- Serve and enjoy these classic Peanut Butter Rice Krispie Treats!

These treats are a delicious combination of crispy cereal, creamy peanut butter, and sweet marshmallows. They are perfect for a quick and easy dessert or snack.

Peanut Butter and Jelly Oat Bars

Ingredients:

For the Oat Base and Crumble:

- 1 and 1/2 cups old-fashioned oats
- 1 cup all-purpose flour
- 1/2 cup packed brown sugar
- 1/2 teaspoon baking powder
- 1/4 teaspoon salt
- 1 cup unsalted butter, cold and cut into small pieces
- 1 teaspoon vanilla extract

For the Peanut Butter and Jelly Filling:

- 1 cup creamy peanut butter
- 1/2 cup fruit preserves or jelly of your choice

Instructions:

Preheat Oven:
- Preheat your oven to 350°F (175°C). Grease or line a 9x9-inch baking pan with parchment paper.

Prepare Oat Base and Crumble:
- In a large mixing bowl, combine the old-fashioned oats, all-purpose flour, brown sugar, baking powder, and salt. Add the cold, cubed butter and vanilla extract. Using a pastry cutter or your fingers, work the mixture until it resembles coarse crumbs.

Set Aside a Portion for Topping:
- Set aside about 1 cup of the oat mixture to use as the crumble topping.

Press Oat Mixture into Pan:
- Press the remaining oat mixture into the bottom of the prepared baking pan, creating an even layer.

Spread Peanut Butter:

- In a small saucepan, warm the creamy peanut butter over low heat until it becomes easily spreadable. Gently spread the peanut butter over the oat base.

Add Jelly or Preserves:
- Spoon the fruit preserves or jelly over the peanut butter layer, spreading it evenly.

Sprinkle Crumble Topping:
- Sprinkle the reserved oat mixture evenly over the jelly layer to create a crumble topping.

Bake:
- Bake in the preheated oven for 25-30 minutes or until the edges are golden brown.

Cool:
- Allow the Peanut Butter and Jelly Oat Bars to cool completely in the pan.

Cut into Bars:
- Once cooled, lift the bars out of the pan using the parchment paper, if used. Cut into squares or bars.

Serve and Enjoy:
- Serve and enjoy these delicious Peanut Butter and Jelly Oat Bars!

These bars are a delightful blend of peanut butter, jelly, and wholesome oats. They make for a tasty snack or a sweet treat for any occasion.

Peanut Butter Cup Milkshake

Ingredients:

- 2 cups vanilla ice cream
- 1/2 cup milk (dairy or plant-based)
- 1/4 cup creamy peanut butter
- 2 tablespoons chocolate syrup
- 1/2 cup crushed peanut butter cups
- Whipped cream for topping (optional)
- Additional peanut butter cups for garnish (optional)

Instructions:

Prepare Peanut Butter Cups:
- Begin by crushing peanut butter cups into small pieces. You can use a food processor or place them in a sealed plastic bag and crush with a rolling pin.

Blend Milkshake:
- In a blender, combine vanilla ice cream, milk, creamy peanut butter, and chocolate syrup. Blend until smooth and creamy.

Add Crushed Peanut Butter Cups:
- Add the crushed peanut butter cups to the blender and pulse briefly to incorporate them into the milkshake.

Pour into Glasses:
- Pour the peanut butter cup milkshake into glasses.

Top with Whipped Cream (Optional):
- If desired, top the milkshake with whipped cream.

Garnish (Optional):
- Garnish with additional crushed peanut butter cups or a drizzle of chocolate syrup for an extra indulgent touch.

Serve Immediately:
- Serve the Peanut Butter Cup Milkshake immediately, using a straw or spoon to enjoy the delicious combination of peanut butter and chocolate.

This milkshake is a delightful treat, combining the rich flavors of peanut butter cups with creamy vanilla ice cream. It's perfect for satisfying your sweet cravings on a warm day or as a special dessert.

Peanut Butter Banana Pancakes

Ingredients:

- 1 cup all-purpose flour
- 2 tablespoons sugar
- 1 teaspoon baking powder
- 1/2 teaspoon baking soda
- 1/4 teaspoon salt
- 1 ripe banana, mashed
- 1/2 cup creamy peanut butter
- 1 cup buttermilk
- 1 large egg
- 1 teaspoon vanilla extract
- Butter or oil for cooking

Optional Toppings:

- Sliced bananas
- Chopped nuts
- Maple syrup

Instructions:

Preheat Griddle or Pan:
- Preheat a griddle or non-stick pan over medium heat.

Mix Dry Ingredients:
- In a large bowl, whisk together the flour, sugar, baking powder, baking soda, and salt.

Combine Wet Ingredients:
- In a separate bowl, mash the ripe banana and mix it with creamy peanut butter, buttermilk, egg, and vanilla extract until well combined.

Combine Wet and Dry Ingredients:
- Pour the wet ingredients into the dry ingredients and stir until just combined. Do not overmix; a few lumps are okay.

Cook Pancakes:

- Grease the griddle or pan with butter or oil. Pour 1/4 cup portions of batter onto the griddle for each pancake. Cook until bubbles form on the surface, then flip and cook the other side until golden brown.

Keep Warm:
- Keep the cooked pancakes warm in a low-temperature oven while you finish cooking the remaining batter.

Serve:
- Serve the Peanut Butter Banana Pancakes with sliced bananas, chopped nuts, and a drizzle of maple syrup if desired.

Enjoy:
- Enjoy these fluffy and flavorful pancakes with the delightful combination of peanut butter and banana!

These Peanut Butter Banana Pancakes are a tasty and wholesome breakfast option that combines the natural sweetness of bananas with the richness of peanut butter. They are sure to be a hit at the breakfast table!

Peanut Butter Granola

Ingredients:

- 3 cups old-fashioned rolled oats
- 1 cup chopped nuts (e.g., almonds, walnuts, or a mix)
- 1/2 cup seeds (e.g., sunflower or pumpkin seeds)
- 1/2 cup shredded coconut (optional)
- 1/2 cup honey or maple syrup
- 1/2 cup creamy peanut butter
- 1/4 cup coconut oil or vegetable oil
- 1 teaspoon vanilla extract
- 1/2 teaspoon salt

Optional Add-ins:

- 1/2 cup dried fruit (e.g., raisins, cranberries, or chopped apricots)

Instructions:

Preheat Oven:
- Preheat your oven to 325°F (163°C). Line a baking sheet with parchment paper.

Mix Dry Ingredients:
- In a large bowl, combine the rolled oats, chopped nuts, seeds, and shredded coconut (if using).

Warm Peanut Butter Mixture:
- In a small saucepan over low heat, warm the honey or maple syrup, peanut butter, coconut oil, vanilla extract, and salt. Stir until well combined and smooth.

Combine Wet and Dry Ingredients:
- Pour the warm peanut butter mixture over the dry ingredients. Stir well to ensure that all the dry ingredients are coated.

Spread on Baking Sheet:
- Spread the mixture evenly onto the prepared baking sheet.

Bake:
- Bake in the preheated oven for 20-25 minutes, or until the granola is golden brown, stirring halfway through to ensure even baking.

Add Dried Fruit (Optional):
- If you're using dried fruit, add it to the granola after removing it from the oven and while it's still warm. Stir to combine.

Cool:
- Allow the granola to cool completely on the baking sheet. It will continue to crisp up as it cools.

Store:
- Once cooled, transfer the Peanut Butter Granola to an airtight container for storage.

Serve and Enjoy:
- Enjoy your homemade Peanut Butter Granola with yogurt, milk, or as a topping for smoothie bowls.

This Peanut Butter Granola is not only delicious but also customizable based on your preferences. Feel free to experiment with different nuts, seeds, or dried fruits to create your perfect blend.

Peanut Butter and Chocolate Mousse

Ingredients:

For the Peanut Butter Mousse:

- 1 cup creamy peanut butter
- 1/2 cup powdered sugar
- 1 cup heavy cream
- 1 teaspoon vanilla extract

For the Chocolate Mousse:

- 6 ounces (about 1 cup) semisweet or bittersweet chocolate, chopped
- 2 tablespoons unsalted butter
- 2 tablespoons brewed coffee (optional)
- 1 1/2 cups heavy cream
- 1/4 cup granulated sugar
- 1 teaspoon vanilla extract

Optional Toppings:

- Chopped peanuts
- Grated chocolate

Instructions:

For the Peanut Butter Mousse:

Whip Peanut Butter and Sugar:
- In a bowl, whip together the creamy peanut butter and powdered sugar until smooth.

Whip Heavy Cream:
- In a separate bowl, whip the heavy cream until stiff peaks form.

Combine and Fold:
- Gently fold the whipped cream into the peanut butter mixture until well combined. Add vanilla extract and continue folding until smooth.

Chill:
- Place the peanut butter mousse in the refrigerator to chill while you prepare the chocolate mousse.

For the Chocolate Mousse:

Melt Chocolate:
- In a heatproof bowl set over simmering water (double boiler), melt the chocolate, butter, and coffee (if using), stirring until smooth. Remove from heat and let it cool slightly.

Whip Heavy Cream:
- In a separate bowl, whip the heavy cream and granulated sugar until stiff peaks form.

Combine and Fold:
- Gently fold the whipped cream into the melted chocolate mixture until well combined. Add vanilla extract and continue folding until smooth.

Layer Mousse:
- Retrieve the peanut butter mousse from the refrigerator. In serving glasses or bowls, layer the chocolate mousse and peanut butter mousse alternately.

Chill:
- Place the layered mousse in the refrigerator to chill for at least 2 hours or until set.

Optional Toppings:
- Before serving, garnish with chopped peanuts or grated chocolate if desired.

Serve and Enjoy:
- Serve the Peanut Butter and Chocolate Mousse chilled. Enjoy the rich and creamy layers of flavor!

This Peanut Butter and Chocolate Mousse is a decadent dessert that combines the nutty goodness of peanut butter with the rich, velvety texture of chocolate mousse. It's perfect for special occasions or when you're craving a luxurious treat.

Peanut Butter Cup Brownie Bites

Ingredients:

For the Brownie Base:

- 1/2 cup unsalted butter, melted
- 1 cup granulated sugar
- 2 large eggs
- 1 teaspoon vanilla extract
- 1/3 cup unsweetened cocoa powder
- 1/2 cup all-purpose flour
- 1/4 teaspoon salt

For the Peanut Butter Cup Filling:

- 1/2 cup creamy peanut butter
- 1/4 cup powdered sugar
- 1/2 teaspoon vanilla extract

For Topping:

- Mini peanut butter cups, unwrapped

Instructions:

Preheat Oven:
- Preheat your oven to 350°F (175°C). Grease a mini muffin tin or line it with mini cupcake liners.

Prepare Brownie Batter:
- In a bowl, combine melted butter and granulated sugar. Add eggs and vanilla extract, mixing well. Stir in cocoa powder, flour, and salt until just combined.

Fill Mini Muffin Tin:
- Spoon the brownie batter into the mini muffin tin, filling each cup about 2/3 full.

Make Peanut Butter Cup Filling:
- In a separate bowl, mix peanut butter, powdered sugar, and vanilla extract until smooth.

Add Peanut Butter Cup Filling:

- Roll small portions of the peanut butter mixture into balls and place one in the center of each brownie cup, pressing it down slightly.

Bake:
- Bake in the preheated oven for about 10-12 minutes or until the brownie bites are set. Avoid overbaking for a fudgy texture.

Top with Mini Peanut Butter Cups:
- While the brownie bites are still warm, gently press a mini peanut butter cup into the center of each bite.

Cool:
- Allow the Peanut Butter Cup Brownie Bites to cool in the mini muffin tin for a few minutes before transferring them to a wire rack to cool completely.

Serve and Enjoy:
- Once cooled, serve and enjoy these delightful Peanut Butter Cup Brownie Bites!

These bite-sized treats are a perfect combination of rich chocolate brownie and creamy peanut butter filling, making them an irresistible dessert for peanut butter cup lovers.

Peanut Butter Banana Ice Cream

Ingredients:

- 4 ripe bananas, peeled, sliced, and frozen
- 2 tablespoons creamy peanut butter
- 1 teaspoon vanilla extract (optional)
- Toppings of your choice (e.g., chopped nuts, chocolate chips, or sliced bananas)

Instructions:

Freeze Bananas:
- Slice the ripe bananas and place the slices in a single layer on a tray or plate. Freeze for at least 2-3 hours or until solid.

Blend Frozen Bananas:
- Place the frozen banana slices in a high-powered blender or food processor. Blend until the bananas become crumbly.

Add Peanut Butter:
- Add the creamy peanut butter to the blender. Continue blending until the mixture becomes smooth and creamy. You may need to stop and scrape down the sides of the blender as needed.

Optional: Add Vanilla Extract:
- If desired, add vanilla extract to enhance the flavor. Blend again until well combined.

Serve:
- Scoop the Peanut Butter Banana Ice Cream into bowls or cones.

Add Toppings:
- Add your favorite toppings, such as chopped nuts, chocolate chips, or sliced bananas.

Enjoy Immediately:
- Serve and enjoy your homemade Peanut Butter Banana Ice Cream immediately!

This easy and healthier alternative to traditional ice cream is not only delicious but also dairy-free and naturally sweetened by the bananas. It's a perfect treat for a hot day or a guilt-free dessert option.

Peanut Butter and Jelly Cupcakes

Ingredients:

For the Cupcakes:

- 1 and 1/2 cups all-purpose flour
- 1 and 1/2 teaspoons baking powder
- 1/4 teaspoon salt
- 1/2 cup unsalted butter, softened
- 1 cup granulated sugar
- 2 large eggs
- 1 teaspoon vanilla extract
- 1/2 cup creamy peanut butter
- 1/2 cup milk

For the Peanut Butter Frosting:

- 1 cup creamy peanut butter
- 1/2 cup unsalted butter, softened
- 2 cups powdered sugar
- 1 teaspoon vanilla extract
- 2-3 tablespoons milk

For the Jelly Filling:

- Your favorite fruit jelly or jam

Instructions:

For the Cupcakes:

Preheat Oven:
- Preheat your oven to 350°F (175°C). Line a cupcake tin with paper liners.

Mix Dry Ingredients:
- In a bowl, whisk together the flour, baking powder, and salt. Set aside.

Cream Butter and Sugar:

- In a large bowl, cream together the softened butter and granulated sugar until light and fluffy.

Add Eggs and Vanilla:
- Beat in the eggs one at a time, then add the vanilla extract and mix well.

Add Peanut Butter:
- Mix in the creamy peanut butter until well combined.

Alternate Dry Ingredients and Milk:
- Gradually add the dry ingredients to the wet ingredients, alternating with the milk. Begin and end with the dry ingredients. Mix until just combined.

Fill Cupcake Liners:
- Spoon the batter into the cupcake liners, filling each about 2/3 full.

Bake:
- Bake in the preheated oven for 18-20 minutes or until a toothpick inserted into the center comes out clean. Allow the cupcakes to cool completely.

For the Peanut Butter Frosting:

Cream Peanut Butter and Butter:
- In a bowl, cream together the creamy peanut butter and softened butter until smooth.

Add Powdered Sugar and Vanilla:
- Gradually add the powdered sugar, beating well after each addition. Add the vanilla extract and continue to mix.

Adjust Consistency:
- If the frosting is too thick, add milk one tablespoon at a time until you reach the desired consistency.

Assembly:

Core Cupcakes:
- Use a cupcake corer or a small spoon to remove a small portion from the center of each cupcake.

Fill with Jelly:
- Fill each cored center with your favorite fruit jelly or jam.

Frost Cupcakes:
- Pipe or spread the Peanut Butter Frosting over the cupcakes.

Decorate (Optional):
- If desired, drizzle a small amount of jelly on top for decoration.

Serve and Enjoy:
- Serve these delightful Peanut Butter and Jelly Cupcakes and enjoy the delicious combination of flavors!

These cupcakes are a fun and tasty twist on the classic peanut butter and jelly combination, perfect for any occasion or as a special treat.

Peanut Butter and Chocolate Pie

Ingredients:

For the Crust:

- 1 and 1/2 cups chocolate cookie crumbs (from about 20 chocolate sandwich cookies)
- 6 tablespoons unsalted butter, melted

For the Peanut Butter Filling:

- 1 cup creamy peanut butter
- 1 cup powdered sugar
- 1/2 cup unsalted butter, softened
- 1 teaspoon vanilla extract
- 1/2 cup heavy cream, whipped to stiff peaks

For the Chocolate Ganache Topping:

- 1 cup semisweet or bittersweet chocolate chips
- 1/2 cup heavy cream
- 2 tablespoons unsalted butter

Optional Toppings:

- Chopped peanuts
- Chocolate shavings

Instructions:

For the Crust:

  Prepare Crust:
  - In a bowl, mix the chocolate cookie crumbs and melted butter until well combined.

  Press into Pie Dish:
  - Press the mixture into the bottom and up the sides of a 9-inch pie dish to form the crust. Use the back of a spoon or a flat-bottomed cup to press it firmly.

Chill:
- Place the crust in the refrigerator to chill while you prepare the filling.

For the Peanut Butter Filling:

Whip Peanut Butter Mixture:
- In a bowl, beat together the creamy peanut butter, powdered sugar, softened butter, and vanilla extract until smooth.

Fold in Whipped Cream:
- Gently fold in the whipped cream until well combined. Be careful not to deflate the whipped cream.

Spread Filling into Crust:
- Spread the peanut butter filling evenly into the chilled crust. Smooth the top with a spatula.

Chill:
- Place the pie in the refrigerator to chill while you prepare the chocolate ganache.

For the Chocolate Ganache Topping:

Heat Chocolate, Cream, and Butter:
- In a heatproof bowl, combine the chocolate chips, heavy cream, and unsalted butter. Heat in the microwave or over a double boiler until the chocolate is melted and the mixture is smooth. Stir until well combined.

Cool Slightly:
- Allow the chocolate ganache to cool slightly before pouring it over the peanut butter filling.

Pour Ganache Over Pie:
- Pour the chocolate ganache over the peanut butter filling, spreading it evenly with a spatula.

Chill:
- Place the pie back in the refrigerator to set for at least 2 hours or until the ganache is firm.

Optional:

Top with Chopped Peanuts and Chocolate Shavings:
- Before serving, you can optionally top the pie with chopped peanuts and chocolate shavings.

Slice and Serve:
- Slice the Peanut Butter and Chocolate Pie and serve chilled. Enjoy the decadent combination of flavors!

This pie is a heavenly treat for peanut butter and chocolate lovers. It combines a rich peanut butter filling with a smooth chocolate ganache, all nestled in a delicious chocolate cookie crust. Perfect for special occasions or any time you crave a delightful dessert!

Peanut Butter and Pretzel Pie

Ingredients:

For the Pretzel Crust:

- 2 cups pretzel crumbs
- 1/2 cup unsalted butter, melted
- 1/4 cup granulated sugar

For the Peanut Butter Filling:

- 1 cup creamy peanut butter
- 8 ounces cream cheese, softened
- 1 cup powdered sugar
- 1 teaspoon vanilla extract
- 1 cup heavy cream, whipped to stiff peaks

For the Chocolate Ganache:

- 1/2 cup semisweet or bittersweet chocolate chips
- 1/2 cup heavy cream

Optional Toppings:

- Chopped pretzels
- Drizzle of melted peanut butter

Instructions:

For the Pretzel Crust:

Preheat Oven:
- Preheat your oven to 350°F (175°C).

Crush Pretzels:
- In a food processor, crush the pretzels into fine crumbs.

Mix Pretzel Crumbs and Sugar:
- In a bowl, combine the pretzel crumbs, melted butter, and granulated sugar. Mix until the crumbs are evenly coated.

Press into Pie Dish:
- Press the pretzel mixture into the bottom and up the sides of a pie dish to form the crust.

Bake:
- Bake the crust in the preheated oven for about 8-10 minutes, or until it is set. Allow it to cool completely.

For the Peanut Butter Filling:

Whip Cream:
- In a bowl, whip the heavy cream until stiff peaks form.

Prepare Peanut Butter Mixture:
- In a separate bowl, beat together the creamy peanut butter, softened cream cheese, powdered sugar, and vanilla extract until smooth.

Fold in Whipped Cream:
- Gently fold the whipped cream into the peanut butter mixture until well combined.

Fill Pretzel Crust:
- Spoon the peanut butter filling into the cooled pretzel crust, spreading it evenly.

For the Chocolate Ganache:

Heat Cream:
- In a saucepan, heat the heavy cream until it just begins to simmer.

Pour Over Chocolate:
- Pour the hot cream over the chocolate chips. Let it sit for a minute, then stir until the chocolate is completely melted and smooth.

Pour Over Peanut Butter Filling:
- Pour the chocolate ganache over the peanut butter filling, spreading it evenly.

Chill:
- Place the pie in the refrigerator to chill for at least 4 hours or until set.

Optional Toppings:

Add Pretzels and Drizzle:
- Before serving, sprinkle chopped pretzels on top and drizzle with melted peanut butter if desired.

Serve and Enjoy:
- Slice and serve this delicious Peanut Butter and Pretzel Pie, savoring the perfect blend of sweet and salty flavors!

This pie is a wonderful combination of creamy peanut butter filling, a crunchy pretzel crust, and a rich chocolate ganache topping. It's a crowd-pleaser that brings together sweet and salty flavors for a delightful dessert.

Peanut Butter and Jelly Smoothie

Ingredients:

- 1 ripe banana, peeled and frozen
- 1 cup frozen mixed berries (strawberries, blueberries, raspberries)
- 2 tablespoons creamy peanut butter
- 1 cup milk (dairy or plant-based)
- 1 tablespoon chia seeds (optional)
- 1-2 tablespoons fruit jelly or jam (your favorite flavor)
- Ice cubes (optional)

Instructions:

Prepare Ingredients:
- Peel and slice the banana before freezing it. Measure out the frozen mixed berries.

Blend Ingredients:
- In a blender, combine the frozen banana, frozen mixed berries, creamy peanut butter, milk, and chia seeds (if using). Add a handful of ice cubes if you prefer a colder smoothie.

Blend Until Smooth:
- Blend the ingredients until smooth and creamy. If the smoothie is too thick, you can add more milk to reach your desired consistency.

Add Jelly or Jam:
- Spoon the fruit jelly or jam into the blender. Pulse a few times or blend briefly to swirl the jelly into the smoothie without fully incorporating it.

Pour and Serve:
- Pour the Peanut Butter and Jelly Smoothie into a glass.

Optional Garnish:
- Garnish with a drizzle of additional peanut butter or a dollop of jelly on top, if desired.

Serve and Enjoy:
- Stir gently and enjoy this delightful Peanut Butter and Jelly Smoothie with the classic flavors of a PB&J sandwich in a refreshing drink!

This smoothie is a great way to enjoy the nostalgic taste of a peanut butter and jelly sandwich in a nutritious and satisfying beverage. Feel free to customize the ingredients to suit your taste preferences.

Peanut Butter Cup Popcorn

Ingredients:

- 10 cups popped popcorn (about 1/2 cup unpopped kernels)
- 1 cup milk chocolate chips or chunks
- 1/2 cup creamy peanut butter
- 1/2 cup powdered sugar
- 1/2 teaspoon vanilla extract
- 1/2 teaspoon salt
- 1 cup mini peanut butter cups, halved (for topping, optional)

Instructions:

Pop the Popcorn:
- Pop the popcorn using your preferred method. Remove any unpopped kernels.

Prepare Peanut Butter Drizzle:
- In a microwave-safe bowl, combine the milk chocolate chips or chunks and creamy peanut butter. Microwave in 20-second intervals, stirring between each, until the mixture is smooth and well combined.

Add Vanilla, Sugar, and Salt:
- Stir in the vanilla extract, powdered sugar, and salt into the peanut butter-chocolate mixture. Mix until smooth.

Drizzle Over Popcorn:
- Place the popped popcorn in a large mixing bowl. Drizzle the peanut butter-chocolate mixture over the popcorn, making sure to coat it evenly. You can use a spatula or your hands to gently toss the popcorn and ensure an even coating.

Optional: Add Mini Peanut Butter Cups:
- If desired, add halved mini peanut butter cups to the popcorn mixture. Toss gently to distribute them evenly.

Let It Set:
- Allow the peanut butter cup popcorn to sit for a few minutes to allow the drizzle to set.

Serve and Enjoy:
- Once the drizzle has set, serve the Peanut Butter Cup Popcorn in a large bowl or portion into individual servings. Enjoy this delightful sweet and savory treat!

This Peanut Butter Cup Popcorn is a fantastic snack for movie nights or special occasions. The combination of popcorn, chocolate, and peanut butter creates a delicious and addictive treat that will be a hit with friends and family.

Peanut Butter and Chocolate Stuffed French Toast

Ingredients:

For the Filling:

- 1/2 cup creamy peanut butter
- 1/4 cup powdered sugar
- 1/2 cup chocolate chips

For the French Toast:

- 8 slices of thick-cut bread (like brioche or challah)
- 4 large eggs
- 1 cup milk
- 1 teaspoon vanilla extract
- Butter or cooking spray for cooking

Optional Toppings:

- Maple syrup
- Sliced bananas
- Chopped nuts
- Whipped cream

Instructions:

For the Filling:

Prepare Peanut Butter Filling:
- In a bowl, mix together the creamy peanut butter and powdered sugar until well combined. Stir in the chocolate chips.

For the French Toast:

Create Sandwiches:
- Lay out 8 slices of bread and spread the peanut butter and chocolate chip mixture on 4 of the slices. Top with the remaining 4 slices to create sandwiches.

Whisk Egg Mixture:

- In a shallow dish, whisk together the eggs, milk, and vanilla extract to create the egg mixture.

Dip and Soak:
- Dip each sandwich into the egg mixture, ensuring that both sides are well-coated. Allow them to soak for a few seconds.

Cook French Toast:
- In a skillet or griddle over medium heat, melt butter or use cooking spray. Cook each side of the sandwiches until golden brown and the chocolate is melted, approximately 3-4 minutes per side.

Serve:
- Remove the stuffed French toast from the skillet and let them rest for a minute. Slice diagonally and serve.

Optional Toppings:
- Top with maple syrup, sliced bananas, chopped nuts, or whipped cream if desired.

Enjoy:
- Serve immediately and enjoy the gooey and delicious Peanut Butter and Chocolate Stuffed French Toast!

This stuffed French toast is a decadent and delightful breakfast or brunch option that combines the richness of peanut butter and chocolate. It's sure to be a hit with anyone who loves the classic flavor pairing of these two ingredients.

Peanut Butter Cup Cookie Bars

Ingredients:

For the Cookie Base:

- 1 cup unsalted butter, softened
- 1 cup granulated sugar
- 1 cup brown sugar, packed
- 2 large eggs
- 1 teaspoon vanilla extract
- 2 cups all-purpose flour
- 1 teaspoon baking powder
- 1/2 teaspoon salt
- 1 and 1/2 cups mini peanut butter cups, chopped

For the Peanut Butter Cup Layer:

- 1 cup creamy peanut butter
- 1/2 cup powdered sugar
- 1 teaspoon vanilla extract

For the Chocolate Ganache:

- 1 cup semisweet or bittersweet chocolate chips
- 1/2 cup heavy cream

Instructions:

For the Cookie Base:

Preheat Oven:
- Preheat your oven to 350°F (175°C). Grease a 9x13-inch baking pan or line it with parchment paper.

Cream Butter and Sugars:
- In a large bowl, cream together the softened butter, granulated sugar, and brown sugar until light and fluffy.

Add Eggs and Vanilla:
- Add the eggs one at a time, beating well after each addition. Stir in the vanilla extract.

Combine Dry Ingredients:
- In a separate bowl, whisk together the flour, baking powder, and salt. Gradually add the dry ingredients to the wet ingredients, mixing until just combined.

Fold in Chopped Peanut Butter Cups:
- Gently fold in the chopped mini peanut butter cups into the cookie dough.

Spread in Pan:
- Spread the cookie dough evenly into the prepared baking pan.

For the Peanut Butter Cup Layer:

Prepare Peanut Butter Filling:
- In a bowl, mix together the creamy peanut butter, powdered sugar, and vanilla extract until smooth.

Spread Peanut Butter Layer:
- Spread the peanut butter mixture over the cookie dough layer in the baking pan.

For the Chocolate Ganache:

Heat Cream:
- In a saucepan, heat the heavy cream until it just begins to simmer.

Pour Over Chocolate:
- Pour the hot cream over the chocolate chips. Let it sit for a minute, then stir until the chocolate is completely melted and smooth.

Spread Chocolate Ganache:
- Spread the chocolate ganache over the peanut butter layer.

Chill:
- Place the pan in the refrigerator to chill for at least 2 hours or until the layers are set.

Slice and Serve:
- Once set, slice into bars and serve. Enjoy these Peanut Butter Cup Cookie Bars!

These cookie bars are a delightful combination of soft cookie base, creamy peanut butter layer, and rich chocolate ganache—a perfect treat for peanut butter cup enthusiasts!

Peanut Butter and Banana Smoothie Bowl

Ingredients:

For the Smoothie Base:

- 2 ripe bananas, frozen
- 1/2 cup creamy peanut butter
- 1 cup Greek yogurt
- 1/2 cup milk (dairy or plant-based)
- 1 tablespoon honey or maple syrup (optional for sweetness)
- 1 teaspoon vanilla extract

Toppings:

- Sliced banana
- Chopped nuts (e.g., almonds, walnuts)
- Granola
- Drizzle of peanut butter
- Chia seeds
- Sliced strawberries or other berries

Instructions:

Prepare Smoothie Base:
- In a blender, combine the frozen bananas, creamy peanut butter, Greek yogurt, milk, honey or maple syrup (if using), and vanilla extract.

Blend Until Smooth:
- Blend the ingredients until smooth and creamy. If the mixture is too thick, you can add more milk to achieve your desired consistency.

Pour into Bowl:
- Pour the smoothie into a bowl.

Add Toppings:
- Arrange your favorite toppings on top of the smoothie bowl. You can get creative with the presentation and add a variety of textures and flavors.

Drizzle with Peanut Butter:
- Finish off by drizzling a bit of extra peanut butter on top.

Serve and Enjoy:
- Serve your Peanut Butter and Banana Smoothie Bowl immediately and enjoy a nutritious and delicious breakfast or snack.

This smoothie bowl is not only tasty but also packed with protein, fiber, and healthy fats. It's a satisfying and energizing way to start your day or to refuel after a workout. Feel free to customize the toppings based on your preferences.

Peanut Butter Cup Mug Cake

Ingredients:

- 4 tablespoons all-purpose flour
- 3 tablespoons granulated sugar
- 2 tablespoons unsweetened cocoa powder
- 1/8 teaspoon baking powder
- a pinch of salt
- 3 tablespoons milk (dairy or plant-based)
- 2 tablespoons creamy peanut butter
- 2 tablespoons vegetable oil or melted butter
- 1/4 teaspoon vanilla extract
- 2 tablespoons chocolate chips
- 1-2 peanut butter cups, chopped (optional, for topping)

Instructions:

Combine Dry Ingredients:
- In a microwave-safe mug, whisk together the flour, sugar, cocoa powder, baking powder, and a pinch of salt.

Add Wet Ingredients:
- Add the milk, creamy peanut butter, vegetable oil or melted butter, and vanilla extract to the mug. Stir until well combined.

Add Chocolate Chips:
- Fold in the chocolate chips into the batter.

Microwave:
- Microwave the mug on high for 1 minute and 30 seconds to 2 minutes, or until the cake has risen and set in the middle. Cooking time may vary based on your microwave's wattage, so adjust accordingly.

Top with Peanut Butter Cups:
- If desired, top the mug cake with chopped peanut butter cups while it's still warm.

Let It Cool for a Moment:
- Allow the mug cake to cool for a minute before enjoying.

Serve and Enjoy:
- Grab a spoon and enjoy your Peanut Butter Cup Mug Cake right from the mug!

This Peanut Butter Cup Mug Cake is a delightful single-serving dessert that's perfect for satisfying sweet cravings in a hurry. Customize it by adding your favorite toppings or enjoy it as is.

Peanut Butter and Jelly Cheesecake

Ingredients:

For the Crust:

- 1 1/2 cups graham cracker crumbs
- 1/3 cup melted butter
- 1/4 cup granulated sugar

For the Cheesecake Filling:

- 4 packages (8 ounces each) cream cheese, softened
- 1 cup granulated sugar
- 4 large eggs
- 1 teaspoon vanilla extract
- 1/2 cup creamy peanut butter

For the Jelly Swirl:

- 1/2 cup fruit jelly or jam (your favorite flavor)

Instructions:

For the Crust:

Preheat Oven:
- Preheat your oven to 325°F (163°C). Grease a 9-inch springform pan.

Mix Crust Ingredients:
- In a bowl, combine graham cracker crumbs, melted butter, and granulated sugar. Press the mixture firmly into the bottom of the prepared springform pan.

Bake Crust:
- Bake the crust in the preheated oven for 10 minutes. Remove from the oven and allow it to cool while preparing the filling.

For the Cheesecake Filling:

Beat Cream Cheese:

- In a large mixing bowl, beat the softened cream cheese until smooth and creamy.

Add Sugar:
- Add the granulated sugar and continue to beat until well combined.

Add Eggs:
- Add the eggs one at a time, beating well after each addition.

Add Vanilla and Peanut Butter:
- Mix in the vanilla extract and creamy peanut butter until the batter is smooth.

Assembling and Baking:

Pour Filling into Crust:
- Pour the cream cheese mixture over the baked crust in the springform pan.

Add Jelly Swirl:
- Drop spoonfuls of fruit jelly or jam onto the surface of the cheesecake filling. Use a knife or skewer to gently swirl the jelly into the batter, creating a marbled effect.

Bake Cheesecake:
- Bake the cheesecake in the preheated oven for about 55-65 minutes or until the center is set, and the edges are slightly golden.

Cool and Refrigerate:
- Allow the cheesecake to cool in the pan on a wire rack. Once cooled, refrigerate for at least 4 hours or overnight.

Serve:
- Once chilled, remove the cheesecake from the springform pan, slice, and serve.

Optional:

- Garnish with additional fruit jelly or fresh berries before serving.

This Peanut Butter and Jelly Cheesecake offers a delicious twist on a classic dessert, combining the rich and creamy texture of cheesecake with the nostalgic flavors of peanut butter and jelly. It's perfect for special occasions or any time you want a delightful treat.

Peanut Butter and Chocolate Covered Strawberries

Ingredients:

- Fresh strawberries, washed and dried
- Creamy peanut butter
- High-quality chocolate (milk, dark, or white chocolate), chopped
- Optional toppings: Chopped nuts, shredded coconut, sprinkles

Instructions:

Prepare Strawberries:
- Ensure that the strawberries are completely dry. Water can cause the chocolate to seize, so pat them dry with paper towels.

Fill Strawberries with Peanut Butter:
- Using a small paring knife or strawberry huller, carefully remove the stems and create a small cavity in each strawberry. Fill each cavity with a small amount of creamy peanut butter.

Melt Chocolate:
- In a heatproof bowl, melt the chopped chocolate. You can do this using a double boiler or by microwaving in short intervals, stirring between each interval until the chocolate is smooth.

Dip Strawberries:
- Holding each strawberry by the stem or using a toothpick, dip it into the melted chocolate, ensuring that it's well-coated.

Place on Parchment Paper:
- Place the chocolate-covered strawberries on a parchment paper-lined tray or plate.

Optional Toppings:
- While the chocolate is still wet, you can sprinkle toppings like chopped nuts, shredded coconut, or sprinkles on the strawberries.

Chill:
- Place the tray in the refrigerator to allow the chocolate to set. This usually takes about 15-20 minutes.

Serve and Enjoy:
- Once the chocolate is set, serve your Peanut Butter and Chocolate Covered Strawberries and enjoy this delicious and elegant treat.

These chocolate-covered strawberries with a peanut butter twist are perfect for special occasions, romantic gestures, or as a delightful treat any time. Customize them with your favorite toppings to add extra flavor and texture.

Peanut Butter Cup Waffles

Ingredients:

For the Waffle Batter:

- 2 cups all-purpose flour
- 2 tablespoons sugar
- 1 tablespoon baking powder
- 1/2 teaspoon salt
- 1 3/4 cups milk
- 1/3 cup vegetable oil
- 2 large eggs
- 1 teaspoon vanilla extract

For the Peanut Butter Cup Swirl:

- 1/2 cup creamy peanut butter
- 1/4 cup powdered sugar
- 1/4 cup milk
- 1 teaspoon vanilla extract
- Mini peanut butter cups, chopped (for topping)

Instructions:

For the Waffle Batter:

Preheat Waffle Iron:
- Preheat your waffle iron according to the manufacturer's instructions.

Mix Dry Ingredients:
- In a large bowl, whisk together the flour, sugar, baking powder, and salt.

Combine Wet Ingredients:
- In a separate bowl, whisk together the milk, vegetable oil, eggs, and vanilla extract.

Combine Wet and Dry Ingredients:
- Pour the wet ingredients into the dry ingredients and stir until just combined. Do not overmix; it's okay if there are some lumps.

For the Peanut Butter Cup Swirl:

Prepare Peanut Butter Mixture:
- In a small bowl, combine the creamy peanut butter, powdered sugar, milk, and vanilla extract. Mix until smooth and well combined.

Assembly:

Swirl Peanut Butter Mixture:
- Drop spoonfuls of the peanut butter mixture onto the waffle batter in the waffle iron. Use a knife or skewer to swirl the peanut butter mixture into the waffle batter.

Cook Waffles:
- Pour the batter onto the preheated waffle iron and cook according to the manufacturer's instructions until golden brown.

Top with Chopped Peanut Butter Cups:
- While the waffles are still warm, sprinkle chopped mini peanut butter cups on top for an extra decadent touch.

Serve:
- Serve the Peanut Butter Cup Waffles warm and enjoy!

These Peanut Butter Cup Waffles are a delicious and indulgent breakfast or brunch option. The combination of fluffy waffles with a peanut butter swirl and chocolatey peanut butter cups makes for a delightful treat.

Peanut Butter and Jelly Overnight Oats

Ingredients:

- 1/2 cup old-fashioned rolled oats
- 1/2 cup milk (dairy or plant-based)
- 2 tablespoons creamy peanut butter
- 1 tablespoon chia seeds
- 1 tablespoon maple syrup or honey
- 1/4 cup fruit jelly or jam (your favorite flavor)
- Fresh berries or sliced banana for topping (optional)

Instructions:

Combine Ingredients:
- In a jar or airtight container, combine rolled oats, milk, creamy peanut butter, chia seeds, and maple syrup.

Mix Well:
- Stir the ingredients well to ensure that the oats are fully coated and the peanut butter is evenly distributed.

Layer with Jelly:
- Spoon the fruit jelly or jam over the oat mixture. You can either stir it in for a more uniform flavor or leave it layered for a swirl effect.

Seal and Refrigerate:
- Seal the jar or container and place it in the refrigerator. Let it sit overnight or for at least 4 hours to allow the oats to absorb the liquid.

Stir Before Serving:
- Before serving, give the overnight oats a good stir to mix the layers and achieve a creamy consistency.

Top with Fresh Fruit:
- Top the oats with fresh berries or sliced banana just before serving for added freshness and flavor.

Enjoy:
- Enjoy your Peanut Butter and Jelly Overnight Oats straight from the refrigerator. No cooking required!

This easy and convenient breakfast option combines the classic flavors of peanut butter and jelly with the convenience of overnight oats. It's a great way to start your day with a delicious and nutritious meal. Feel free to customize the recipe with your favorite toppings and enjoy a quick and satisfying breakfast.

Peanut Butter and Chocolate Popsicles

Ingredients:

- 1 cup creamy peanut butter
- 1/4 cup powdered sugar (adjust to taste)
- 1 teaspoon vanilla extract
- 1 1/2 cups chocolate milk (store-bought or homemade)
- 1/4 cup chocolate chips (optional)
- Popsicle molds and sticks

Instructions:

Prepare Peanut Butter Mixture:
- In a bowl, combine the creamy peanut butter, powdered sugar, and vanilla extract. Mix until smooth and well combined. Taste and adjust the sweetness by adding more powdered sugar if needed.

Melt Chocolate Chips (Optional):
- If using chocolate chips, melt them in the microwave or using a double boiler until smooth.

Layer the Popsicle Molds:
- Start by spooning a layer of the peanut butter mixture into the bottom of each popsicle mold.

Add Chocolate Layer:
- If using melted chocolate chips, drizzle a bit over the peanut butter layer in each mold. If not, proceed to the next step.

Continue Layering:
- Continue alternating layers of peanut butter mixture and chocolate until you fill each popsicle mold.

Insert Popsicle Sticks:
- Place popsicle sticks into each mold, making sure they are centered in the mixture.

Freeze:
- Place the popsicle molds in the freezer and let them freeze for at least 4-6 hours or until fully set.

Unmold and Enjoy:

- Once the popsicles are completely frozen, remove them from the molds by running them under warm water for a few seconds. Enjoy your Peanut Butter and Chocolate Popsicles!

These homemade popsicles are a delicious and refreshing treat, combining the rich flavors of peanut butter and chocolate. They're perfect for a hot day or as a sweet and satisfying dessert. Feel free to customize the recipe by adding chopped nuts or other toppings for extra crunch.

Peanut Butter Cup Ice Cream Cake

Ingredients:

For the Crust:

- 2 cups chocolate cookie crumbs (you can use crushed chocolate sandwich cookies)
- 1/2 cup unsalted butter, melted

For the Ice Cream Layer:

- 1.5 quarts chocolate ice cream, softened
- 1 cup peanut butter cups, chopped

For the Peanut Butter Layer:

- 1 cup creamy peanut butter
- 1 cup powdered sugar
- 1/2 cup unsalted butter, softened
- 1 teaspoon vanilla extract

For the Chocolate Ganache:

- 1 cup semisweet chocolate chips
- 1/2 cup heavy cream

Optional Toppings:

- Additional peanut butter cups, chopped
- Chopped nuts
- Whipped cream

Instructions:

For the Crust:

Preheat Oven:
- Preheat your oven to 350°F (175°C).

Mix Crust Ingredients:
- In a bowl, combine the chocolate cookie crumbs and melted butter. Mix until the crumbs are evenly coated.

Press into Pan:
- Press the mixture into the bottom of a springform pan to form the crust. Bake in the preheated oven for about 10 minutes. Allow it to cool completely.

For the Ice Cream Layer:

Soften Ice Cream:
- Let the chocolate ice cream soften at room temperature.

Add Peanut Butter Cups:
- Once softened, fold in the chopped peanut butter cups. Spread this mixture over the cooled crust. Place the pan back in the freezer to firm up.

For the Peanut Butter Layer:

Prepare Peanut Butter Mixture:
- In a bowl, beat together the creamy peanut butter, powdered sugar, softened butter, and vanilla extract until smooth.

Spread Over Ice Cream Layer:
- Spread the peanut butter mixture over the chocolate ice cream layer in the pan. Return to the freezer to set.

For the Chocolate Ganache:

Prepare Ganache:
- In a saucepan, heat the heavy cream until it just begins to simmer. Pour the hot cream over the chocolate chips in a bowl. Let it sit for a minute, then stir until smooth.

Pour Over Peanut Butter Layer:
- Pour the chocolate ganache over the peanut butter layer, spreading it evenly.

Final Freeze:
- Return the cake to the freezer and let it freeze until completely set.

Optional Toppings:

> Decorate and Serve:
> - Before serving, decorate the top with additional chopped peanut butter cups, chopped nuts, or whipped cream if desired.
>
> Slice and Enjoy:
> - Once fully set, remove the cake from the springform pan, slice, and enjoy your delicious Peanut Butter Cup Ice Cream Cake!

This ice cream cake is a crowd-pleaser, combining the classic flavors of peanut butter and chocolate in a cool and creamy dessert. It's perfect for celebrations or any time you crave a sweet and indulgent treat.

Peanut Butter and Banana Quesadilla

Ingredients:

- 1 large flour tortilla
- 2 tablespoons creamy peanut butter
- 1 banana, sliced
- 1 tablespoon honey
- 1/2 teaspoon ground cinnamon
- Butter or cooking spray for cooking

Instructions:

Prepare Ingredients:
- Lay out the flour tortilla and have the peanut butter, sliced banana, honey, and ground cinnamon ready.

Spread Peanut Butter:
- Spread the creamy peanut butter evenly over one half of the tortilla, leaving a small border around the edges.

Add Banana Slices:
- Arrange the sliced banana evenly over the peanut butter side of the tortilla.

Drizzle with Honey:
- Drizzle honey over the banana slices and sprinkle ground cinnamon on top.

Fold and Press:
- Fold the tortilla in half, covering the banana side with the peanut butter side.

Cook on Stovetop:
- Heat a skillet or griddle over medium heat. Add a small amount of butter or use cooking spray to coat the surface.

Cook Quesadilla:
- Place the folded quesadilla on the hot skillet and cook for 2-3 minutes on each side or until the tortilla is golden brown and the filling is warm.

Slice and Serve:
- Remove the quesadilla from the skillet and let it cool for a moment. Slice it into wedges and serve.

Optional: Serve with Ice Cream or Yogurt:

- For an extra treat, serve the Peanut Butter and Banana Quesadilla with a scoop of vanilla ice cream or a dollop of Greek yogurt.

Enjoy:
- Enjoy this delightful Peanut Butter and Banana Quesadilla as a quick and tasty snack or dessert!

This quesadilla combines the classic combination of peanut butter and banana in a warm and gooey treat. It's a simple recipe that's perfect for satisfying your sweet cravings. Feel free to customize by adding a sprinkle of chopped nuts or chocolate chips if desired.

Peanut Butter Cup Cheesecake Brownies

Ingredients:

For the Brownie Layer:

- 1/2 cup (1 stick) unsalted butter
- 1 cup granulated sugar
- 2 large eggs
- 1 teaspoon vanilla extract
- 1/3 cup unsweetened cocoa powder
- 1/2 cup all-purpose flour
- 1/4 teaspoon salt
- 1/4 teaspoon baking powder

For the Cheesecake Layer:

- 8 ounces cream cheese, softened
- 1/4 cup granulated sugar
- 1 large egg
- 1/2 teaspoon vanilla extract

Additional Ingredients:

- 1 cup mini peanut butter cups, halved
- 1/4 cup chocolate chips (optional, for drizzling)

Instructions:

For the Brownie Layer:

Preheat Oven:
- Preheat your oven to 350°F (175°C). Grease or line a square baking pan.

Melt Butter:
- In a microwave-safe bowl, melt the butter.

Mix Wet Ingredients:

- In a mixing bowl, combine the melted butter with sugar, eggs, and vanilla extract. Mix until well combined.

Add Dry Ingredients:
- Sift in the cocoa powder, all-purpose flour, salt, and baking powder. Mix until just combined.

Spread in Pan:
- Spread the brownie batter evenly in the prepared baking pan.

For the Cheesecake Layer:

Prepare Cheesecake Batter:
- In another bowl, beat together the softened cream cheese, sugar, egg, and vanilla extract until smooth.

Layer Cheesecake on Brownie Batter:
- Spoon dollops of the cheesecake batter onto the brownie batter in the pan. Use a knife to swirl the two batters together for a marbled effect.

Add Peanut Butter Cups:
- Sprinkle the halved mini peanut butter cups over the batter.

Bake:
- Bake in the preheated oven for 30-35 minutes or until a toothpick inserted into the center comes out with moist crumbs.

Cool:
- Allow the brownies to cool completely in the pan on a wire rack.

Optional Chocolate Drizzle:

Melt Chocolate (Optional):
- If desired, melt chocolate chips in the microwave or using a double boiler.

Drizzle Over Brownies:
- Drizzle the melted chocolate over the cooled brownies for an extra touch.

Chill and Slice:
- Optionally, chill the brownies in the refrigerator for easier slicing. Once chilled, cut into squares and serve.

These Peanut Butter Cup Cheesecake Brownies are a delightful combination of rich chocolate brownie, creamy cheesecake, and the sweet crunch of peanut butter cups. They make for a decadent and irresistible treat!

Peanut Butter and Chocolate Pudding

Ingredients:

For the Chocolate Pudding:

- 1/2 cup granulated sugar
- 1/4 cup unsweetened cocoa powder
- 3 tablespoons cornstarch
- 1/4 teaspoon salt
- 2 1/2 cups milk
- 1 teaspoon vanilla extract
- 4 ounces dark chocolate, chopped

For the Peanut Butter Pudding:

- 1/2 cup granulated sugar
- 3 tablespoons cornstarch
- 1/4 teaspoon salt
- 2 1/2 cups milk
- 1 teaspoon vanilla extract
- 1/2 cup creamy peanut butter

Optional Toppings:

- Whipped cream
- Chopped peanuts
- Chocolate shavings

Instructions:

For the Chocolate Pudding:

Combine Dry Ingredients:
- In a saucepan, whisk together sugar, cocoa powder, cornstarch, and salt.

Add Milk:
- Gradually whisk in the milk until the mixture is smooth and well combined.

Cook Over Medium Heat:
- Cook the mixture over medium heat, whisking constantly, until it starts to thicken.

Add Chocolate:
- Add the chopped dark chocolate and continue whisking until the chocolate is melted, and the pudding is thickened.

Remove from Heat:
- Remove from heat and stir in vanilla extract. Let the chocolate pudding cool for a few minutes.

For the Peanut Butter Pudding:

Combine Dry Ingredients:
- In a separate saucepan, whisk together sugar, cornstarch, and salt.

Add Milk:
- Gradually whisk in the milk until the mixture is smooth and well combined.

Cook Over Medium Heat:
- Cook the mixture over medium heat, whisking constantly, until it starts to thicken.

Add Peanut Butter:
- Add the creamy peanut butter and continue whisking until the peanut butter is fully incorporated, and the pudding is thickened.

Remove from Heat:
- Remove from heat and stir in vanilla extract. Let the peanut butter pudding cool for a few minutes.

Assembly:

Layer Puddings:
- In serving glasses or bowls, layer the chocolate pudding and peanut butter pudding alternately.

Chill:
- Cover and refrigerate the layered pudding for at least 2-3 hours or until fully chilled and set.

Serve:
- Before serving, optionally top with whipped cream, chopped peanuts, or chocolate shavings.

Enjoy:

- Serve and enjoy this delightful Peanut Butter and Chocolate Pudding!

This layered pudding combines the rich flavors of chocolate and peanut butter for a delicious and satisfying dessert. It's a perfect treat for those who love the classic combination of these two beloved ingredients.